T0149424

TEA TIME

LIFE'S DIFFICULT QUESTIONS

RICHARD BRADEN

IUNIVERSE, INC.
NEW YORK   BLOOMINGTON

Tea Time
Life's Difficult Questions

iUniverse books may be ordered through booksellers or by contacting:

iUniverse
1663 Liberty Drive
Bloomington, IN 47403
www.iuniverse.com
1-800-Authors (1-800-288-4677)

ISBN: 978-1-4401-6747-8 (sc)
ISBN: 978-1-4401-6748-5 (ebk)

Printed in the United States of America

iUniverse rev. date: 9/8/2009

Other Books by Richard Braden:

Reunions, 1999

Lori's Jeep, 2000

The Seventh Bridge, 2001

My Piece of Hollywood, 2001

The Archer House Mystery, 2002

Harriet Reddy, 2002

Milkman, 2002

South Pass, 2002

Testosterone, 2002

Escape From Europe, 2002

Yellow Fever, 2006

A Short Walk to the Poorhouse, 2006

To Live Again, 2006

Fools' Gold, 2006

Cowboys and Indians, 2008

Promontory, 2008

The Big Ditch, 2008

CONTENTS

INTRODUCTION

This is not a children's or teenagers' story, but it definitely 'hits home' where adults are concerned. When you are young you accept the wisdom of the elders, but when you pass the 'empty nester' stage you are forced to look at life from a different perspective. Cold reason begins to replace what some refer to as 'faith' in your mind. This story is fictional but the lives of several real people are included here. The two main characters have firm convictions about several issues, to include politics, love, war, economics, life styles, and religion. So be ready to either cheer for or against the positions taken in this book.

This is a story about two old soldiers in their late fifties, both ex-army men, who have retired from their military services and are soon planning to fully retire from business and industry so they can enter their 'golden years'. One is an American, a retired Major from the U. S. Army, living in Denver, Colorado with his wife of 38 years, Carlie. His name is Bryan Wetherington. He brought a few incidental chest metals with him into retirement from the U. S. Army, but none are worthy of note.

The second soldier is Timothy O'Doul, a citizen of the United Kingdom (UK), a retired Major from the Royal Army, living in Edinburgh, Scotland with his wife of 39 years, Helen. Major O'Doul also has his share of insignificant metals awarded to him by the Crown. The two men have known each other since the glory days of the 'First Gulf War', the battles fought in Iraq in the early 1990s to put down Saddam Hussein. They met in Basra soon after the Iraqi Republican Guard capitulated and President George Bush, as the Commander of United Nations Forces in the Persian Gulf, declared an end of hostilities and sent the UN forces home.

The two men spent most of their military days in armored units, the behemoth 'panzers' of the twentieth and twenty-first century. They became acquainted because the U. S. Army Abrams heavy tank and the British Challenger I heavy tank used so many common parts. The two men became the central exchange point between the British and U. S. forces for tank parts in Iraq, which were in short supply in the deserts of the Arabian Peninsula. The puts and takes of parts-swapping were supposed to be settled after the war, but the British and American troops parted company so quickly after the war that there never was a final who-owes-who reconciliation. On behalf of the Prime Minister of the United Kingdom and the President of the United States, the two soldiers agreed to buy each-other one long, warm beer each at a GI hangout in Basra, clank the glasses together, and call it a war. The actual buyer of the two beers was a Canadian Lieutenant who was glad to see both senior officers leave, since, upon their departures, he became the commander of the Basra parts depot.

Fourteen years passed, and the two men corresponded with each other, first in letters written on lightweight airmail stationery, and now in emails that made their way from continent to continent in a couple of hours. It was easy to pass 'text' through the early days of the internet, but not so easy to pass graphics, since most internet companies chopped off any attachments that were over 500 or 600 K in size. But there have been improvements lately, and the two men began to send pictures of themselves and their spouses half-way around the world in milliseconds at no cost.

Then, one day in 2005, Timothy O'Doul sent a special email to Bryan Wetherington, imploring him to come to Scotland and attend a two-man, week long, Persian Gulf War fourteenth year reunion. At first Bryan was hesitant to attend, having blown all his United Airlines frequent flyer miles on a trip to New York City for himself and his wife, Carlie. But Carlie read a lot more into Timothy's email, and prevailed upon Bryan to make the trip to the UK.

This is their story.

CHAPTER 1, AN INVITATION

Bryan had no sooner walked in the house from the garage when he was intercepted by Carlie, who was holding a sheet of printer paper with a short message printed on it. "You got a note from Timothy today," she said as she handed him the sheet. "He wants you to visit him in the UK."

Bryan read the note, and then laid it carefully on the kitchen table. "I wish he had brought up this matter six months ago, before we spent all our frequent flyer miles to visit Russell and his family on Long Island. The only way we could go now would be to buy full-fare tourist tickets from here to Heathrow, and I'm not about to spring for that right now."

Carlie picked up the message from the table and waved it under Bryan's nose. "This is no simple request for you to visit, Bryan," she asserted. "Timothy wants you to come, and he wants you to come now. If I recall right, he is only a year older than you are, so this is not some kind of a splurge to join the ranks of the geriatric crowd. Beside, you would only have to buy one airline ticket – I will not be making the trip."

"Why not?" Bryan asked.

"Because Eileen needs me badly for the next few months while she tries to recover from her automobile accident," was the reply. Eileen had been smacked (the proper automotive term is 't-boned') by a young man who ran a red light downtown and hit Eileen's car as she was coming home from downtown Denver. Eileen's left elbow and hand took a beating, as did her left thigh. She was able to go back to work now, her being a physical therapist and all that, but there was an immediate need for someone to take the two grandchildren to the local nursery school early every weekday morning and pick them up in the afternoon. Eileen's husband, Roger, was a fireman and his hours were totally irregular.

"You don't want to go to England?," Bryan asked.

"It's not a case of whether I want to go or don't want to go," Carlie replied. "I have to be here in this place until Eileen recovers fully, and that may be several months from now."

"I'll call and see how much it costs," Bryan said.

"Don't bother," was Carlie's swift reply. "United has a big sale going on right now, and you can fly to Heathrow and back for under $400.00. If you don't want to fly United, British Airways is also advertising low off-season fares to the UK also. This is the perfect time to fly to England."

Bryan could tell that he was pretty well 'setup' on this event. Carlie wanted him to go to England and Timothy also wanted him to go to England. Was there something that they knew that he didn't?

"I'll think about it," was Bryan's reply.

"Don't think too long," Carlie returned. "The sale ends in two days."

"I wonder if my Passport has expired," Bryan mentioned.

"Nope," was Carlie's reply. "You have two years left on the old one. That will not be a problem."

Carlie continued with, "Who is Brigadier Galliard-Trimble?"

Bryan looked at the message from Timothy closely. "Brigadier Galliard-Trimble was probably the last UN soldier to die in the Gulf War," Bryan replied. "He was O'Doul's Corps commander and he was a bit of a historian. Several days after the fighting stopped he and his driver took a trip to a famous old battlefield of 3000 years earlier, just southwest of Basra. While the Brigadier was looking at something close to the Land Rover, his driver, Hoffman, walked a hundred feet or so away to urinate, and at that time a tank shell sent the Land Rover and the Brigadier into the next world. Hoffman hid amongst the rocks and waited for help. O'Doul sensed that something must have gone wrong on the Brigadier's visit when he did not return for the evening meal, and O'Doul and a bunch of Tommies went searching for him. They found Hoffman, who told them what had happened, and they found a revetment about 500 yards north of the Land Rover that had concealed a Republican Guard tank. The tank commander must have hidden there for several days while British tanks passed on either side of his hiding place, and then he fired one last shot to kill one more enemy. Then he pulled out of the revetment and headed for Baghdad."

Bryan continued with, "The first time I met O'Doul at the supply depot, the Union Jack was flying at half-mast, in honor of the Brigadier. There were British tanks all around the depot, which was also the Corps headquarters. After O'Doul and I finished our business, he asked me to stay for tea. They were going to have a special commemorative service for the Brigadier, and I was invited. The outside temperature must have been at least a hundred degrees when we went into the Corps snack bar for tea, and we both drank the tea in silence. There were huge fans in every corner of the room, blowing air to cool the place, but the air was so hot that the 'cooling' air didn't have much affect. Anyway, the Chaplain came in, most of the staff followed, and we all said goodbye to the Brigadier. Hoffman was extremely lucky – he wasn't even scratched when the shell went off. There was nothing left of the Land Rover or the General."

Bryan ended the explanation with, "Every time I returned to the Depot, O'Doul insisted that we take time out for tea, and I agreed."

The closing line on Timothy O'Doul's email message was, "Come to Edinburgh and we'll drink a pint in honor of Galliard-Trimble."

❧   ❧   ❧

A week later Bryan received a confirmation email from United, reminding him that he should bring a copy of the email to the airport the day he departed. The low fare was good on Wednesdays and Thursdays only, so Bryan chose to fly east on a Wednesday and return eight days later from his trip 'over the pond.' To make the occasion more festive, Carlie took him to the local shopping mall and bought him a new dark blue roll-around suitcase that was large enough to hold a pair of pants folded over one time. His old suitcase was much smaller, and required a tri-fold of pants to fit inside. It also required that a suit coat be folded over inside to allow the zipper to close, so his suits always looked like rolled rags when he arrived at his destination. Since Bryan took very few clothes with him on a trip, the one suitcase was sufficient for the eight-day stay. Bryan usually took a briefcase with him on business trips, but this was no business trip. This was a holiday, and Bryan was going to enjoy every minute of it!

CHAPTER 2, HEATHROW

Bryan was not a large person. He stood only five feet nine inches tall so it was easy for him to fit into a tourist-class airline seat, normally. He had kept his U. S. Army readiness weight at 170 pounds, so seat width was not a problem either. But the overseas airliners always 'scooted' the seats up even closer for the long trip (which made the tourists wonder about it all) and Bryan found his knees bumping into the seat in front of him. He wondered if the airline could have charged ten dollars more and added another inch to the space between the seat rows. Maybe this was a subtle hint that he should fly first-class next time.

He was flanked on either side by small, elderly ladies who took up very little room. Bryan could appreciate the extra space because he had been caught in the reverse situation on several occasions when he was flying business-class, having been assigned a seat between two young men who looked like linebackers for the Denver Broncos. They each needed their seat width plus about four inches to pull their shoulders back and relax during the flight, leaving Bryan with just enough room to suffocate. The secret in this case was to slide down as low as possible in the seat and place his shoulders underneath their shoulders, such that they fitted together like a jigsaw puzzle. If the flight was short he could spend part of the trip standing at the back end of the airplane waiting for one of the restrooms to come available. The rolling movement of airplanes always made him feel 'loosey-goosey' and any liquid that he swallowed while on board went immediately to his bladder and fussed at him relentlessly.

On this trip across the Atlantic Ocean he found that he was not the only one in his row who needed to visit the restrooms frequently. For several hours he and the two ladies exchanged pleasantries and moved in and out of the row to allow one of their party to visit the back of the airplane. It was the closest thing to synchronized exercise that one could find on a modern jumbo jet.

When you fly east, nighttime comes very quickly. You are flying in a direction opposed to the sun's movement, so the aircraft moves into the dark half of the world quickly. Once the aircraft reaches its cruising altitude there is little to be seen out the side windows. Most people pull the curtain down across the window, as if leaving it open would allow too much light into the cabin. Lowering the curtain is probably a good idea though – can you imagine how you would feel if you looked out into that emptiness of darkened space and saw something either coming toward you or flying along with you? It's the kind of thing that would make you want to visit the restroom again, quickly.

Passing over the American east coast in the nighttime is also an unusual experience. There is not a single darkened spot anywhere on the horizon. Everyone east of Chicago turns on their lights and lets you know that they are preparing for the night. An aircraft that is flying non-stop from Denver to London chooses a flight path far to the north of New York and Boston, so the mirage of lights finally dies and the only objects seen below are the Maritime Provinces and isolated patches of light from places like Iceland. Once the pilot tells you that Shannon, Ireland is just ahead, you know that Heathrow cannot be far away. In the old days, Shannon, Ireland was a classic jump-off spot for aircraft flying to the USA from the Continent, but now little Shannon (along with the Azores islands) are forgotten by the modern traveler.

A flight from Denver to Heathrow takes many hours, so the passengers have a lot of time to pass along the way. Some people have discovered ways to sleep on an airplane, and others have not. Most passengers on a nine or ten hour flight will pass out eventually from pure exhaustion. Bryan was a non-sleeper, so he had plenty of time to think about the years that he had spent in the Army, first as an artilleryman (gun runner), and later as an armored person (a grinder). Bryan knew exactly why he had transferred from the artillery to the armored when he did – he didn't like to walk. The armored soldiers ride everywhere they go. Artillery soldiers ride a lot also, but the infantry is always left out in the cold (or the hot, as the case may be). The GIs who have the softest jobs in the military are the Navy people – everyone knows that.

Riding along on a ship is a lot of fun. Only infantry GIs have to dig holes. But Bryan didn't like the idea of living in a 'large tin can in the middle of an ocean'. Beside, he was not a very good swimmer.

He had chosen the artillery out of ignorance originally, since the day he enlisted for military service he could have chosen any of the combat arms -- infantry, artillery, or armored. He knew later that he should have picked 'armored' the first time, but there was no one around to advise him. He knew that he didn't want to be in the infantry, but it was a toss-up between the artillery and the armored. The first chance he got, he switched from the artillery to the armored and stayed there. For one thing, it helped to be a small person in the armored divisions because tanks are not that big inside. A really big person would find it 'cramped' inside a tank. All armored soldiers sweat a lot – it's just one of the pitfalls of the business.

Bryan knew that Timothy O'Doul had started out in the British 'armoured', and never left it. Timothy was about the same size as Bryan – maybe an inch taller at the most. Both were slim, both had been raised in agricultural communities, and both enlisted at the lowest rank in the military, a 'private'. The fact that both of them had worked their way through the maze of military promotions to become a 'field grade officer' (a major) was also exciting to them both. There were plenty of military academy graduates who passed through the rank of 'major' early in their careers, aiming for the top general or admiral slots. But these academy grads were a class unto themselves, and everyone knew it. All that the Bryan Wetheringtons and Timothy O'Douls of this world could hope for was a series of smaller promotions in a reasonable length of time. They also knew that there had to be some wars around that they could participate in – else they would be forgotten on promotion days. It was a little sad that one had to hope for a cataclysmic event like a war to promote one's own self respect and social esteem.

Of course, everyone in the U. S. Army knew that General of the Army Dwight David Eisenhower had been a First Lieutenant for 21 years before his big break came. That 'big break' was World War II. They also knew that if General MacArthur had had his way, Eisenhower would never have been promoted past 'Corporal, E3'. But MacArthur was an asshole and everyone knew it. It took a president, Harry S. Truman, to put MacArthur in his place. Harry was a real 'pistol' – no doubt about that. As a soldier, Bryan Wetherington could never be angry with Harry Ass Truman. He called them the way he saw them.

During the years that Bryan and Timothy had corresponded, many subjects were discussed. But making rank or *not* making rank was not one of them. Both men knew that even if you did the best job you were capable of, there was always a good chance that you would be left behind when promotions were passed out. The military is that way. Some fully qualified, knowledgeable, hard-bitten soldiers are always left behind when the train leaves the station – a soldier's pedigree (military academy, Virginia Military, Texas A & M, The Citadel, etc.) is his/her's most valuable asset. Lord help the ROTC graduates who become serious about a military career. At the bottom of this administrative pyramid is a group of men and women who have an undergraduate degree from some USA college, but no 'ROTC' rights to membership, and no parents or grandparents who served in the last war as Generals or Admirals. These are the soldiers who 'pull themselves up by their bootstraps'. Bryan Wetherington and Timothy O'Doul were bootstrap pullers. No matter how long and how hard they worked to gain a place in the military officer corps, they were always referred to as 'ninety-day wonders' by the rest of the military community.

❦   ❦   ❦

When the pilot announced that the airplane was going into a gentle glide to prepare for landing at Heathrow, everyone on board was glad. The sun had already come up in the east so an entire night had passed by in a blur. A lot of the passengers were thinking about reaching their hotels as quickly as possible so they could 'sleep off' the affects of the long airplane ride. Others (mostly the young ones) were itching for some immediate action in London, which they understood was second to no other city on the earth for around-the-clock entertainment. They had been told that London had everything that New York City had, and then some.

No matter how 'suave' one wishes to appear, there is always a collected sigh of relief when the landing gear of a huge aircraft settles down on the pavement and the aircraft begins to roll toward the lights of the airport. There was a gentle rain falling when they landed and made their way to the assigned gate. It would have seemed improper for the rain *not* to be falling when they arrived. After all, this was England, with London, and 'Camelot'. Bryan remembered that in Camelot, rain was allowed to fall only during the night. This particular morning there was just enough light from the sky to erase the effects of 'night'.

Bryan had arranged to meet Timothy and Helen at the baggage carousels. It took a while to de-plane and make one's way to the baggage area because the airport was filled with people who had big plans for the day. Half were rushing to get onto an airplane and the other half were rushing to get away from an airplane. Bryan had not seen Timothy O'Doul in fourteen years, so he hoped that he would not be too hard to spot. Timothy had helped him out in the identification process by mentioning that he walked with a cane in his right hand and he would be wearing a large red, yellow, and green tophat nearly 18 inches tall. It was the sort of hat that Dr. Seuss had placed on the 'Grinch Who Stole Christmas'. This hat had been presented to him by their youngest grandchild who was a Dr. Seuss fan.

By the time Bryan found his single piece of luggage and popped the dragging handle out of its resting place in the bag, the O'Douls had not made an appearance. Bryan had suggested to the O'Douls that he rent a car at Heathrow and drive up to Edinburgh, but Timothy was opposed to any of that. "You better stay off our major highways – you Yanks have some bad habits when it comes to driving, especially when you come to a roundabout" Timothy wrote. Bryan knew exactly what Timothy was referring to because he remembered that Timothy insisted on driving on the left side of the street when the two of them drove in Basra so many years ago. There was no problem with that sort of thing in 1991 because there were no other vehicles in Iraq to be seen anywhere. Bryan tried to remember if the vehicles in Iraq drove on the left side or the right side now – not that it made any difference. He had no desire to visit Iraq again.

Suddenly, there was a tug at Bryan's left arm, and he turned around to face a lady who was about the same size and age as his wife, Carlie. She looked him straight in the eye and introduced herself. "I'm Helen O'Doul," she said. "Timothy is at the train station on the other side of the airport center, holding a place for us so we can catch the ten o'clock train to Edinburgh. Please follow me." Then she added, "Welcome to the UK. We have had a wonderful Spring here so far."

So Bryan followed Helen, who moved quickly. They made their way up and over several stairs, escalators, and one elevator. Then they reached a large train station platform that Hercule Perot' would have loved. As soon as they reached the platform, Bryan spied the Dr. Seuss hat in the crowd. He moved toward the hat, and found a man below the hat that looked much like himself – older and greyer than he remembered but thin-looking, with lots of hair. He certainly had a lot more hair than Bryan had. They embraced and both men started speaking at the same time.

"I'm glad you got here when you did," Timothy told him. "You can see all the people in line to get on the express train to Edinburgh. Of course, it's a big train, so we won't have any problem finding a compartment. We are traveling Second Class, which is not quite as good as First Class, but if Second Class is good enough for 'Harry Potter', than it certainly is good enough for us.

"You have seen some of the Harry Potter movies then?" Bryan asked. Both of the O'Douls bobbed their heads in the affirmative. "I hope that you Yanks will remember that Harry Potter is a British gentleman and a scholar," Timothy said. "We want to make sure that he is not 'Americanized' in the future."

"That will never happen," Bryan assured him. "To get on the train to Edinburgh, do we climb up the steps of the car like they did in the movie 'Around the World in 80 Days', or do we dash ourselves against a post like Harry Potter and the other students did when they returned to 'Hogwarts'?"

"More like '80 days'," Helen answered. "Those granite posts in the middle of the walkway are pretty unforgiving if you run into them." Soon the line began to move and twenty minutes later the three were seated in a train compartment, awaiting the first lurch of the locomotive as it pulled out of the station. "You will really like this express train," Timothy mentioned. "It only makes one stop between here and Edinburgh, in Manchester. The local train makes about a dozen stops along the way and arrives in Edinburgh about two hours after the Express."

Soon the train pulled away from the station and Timothy began to chit-chat about the beautiful green countryside that they were passing through. Denver has pale-green foliage, but the southern UK has deep green foliage that puts the western states to shame. Soon, Bryan began to get very warm and tingly inside, and he knew that sleep was not far away. He remembers Helen putting a blanket over him and he muttered a 'thank you' before the bottom dropped out and he was lifted into dreamland.

The only thing that woke him up was the lurch of the train. It was hard to tell what time it was, but it had to be past noon. Apparently they were in Manchester. When he looked around he found that Helen and Timothy were also covered with blankets and they too were in some state of sleep. There was no rain, but a heavy layer of clouds sheltered the sun. Helen got up and left the compartment. She returned in a couple of minutes and announced that someone had left some debris on the track just short of Manchester and the train was waiting for it to be cleared. "At least we didn't bash a cow," she added. Five minutes later they were on their way again. "We will be in Edinburgh in another two hours," she explained to Bryan.

As one travels from south to north in the UK one cannot help but notice that the deep greenery of the south is slowly replaced with scattered greenery and eventually with rock formations. It is no surprise that the first 'Brits' chose the southern part of the island to make their homes and their living. Those who chose to live at the northern end of the island were a hardy people – they had to be to survive an unforgiving climate with a short growing season and much less rain than the south of the island experienced. They also had to deal with the occasional invasions of the Nordic tribes. It was not surprising that the Nordic tribes could make their way to the UK in boats – what was surprising was how they ever found their way back home after they pillaged the UK countryside. Compasses had not been invented yet, or so the story goes. This was the third time that Bryan had come to Scotland, and every time he marveled at how the natives were able to 'farm' or 'ranch' in this climate. There were few cattle of course, but there were an untold number of sheep and goats. There was not the first piece of land wasted – every spot of exposed earth grew something. The houses were grouped together so the land left for agriculture was maximized. Seeing this land again made him think about the public television series that he had loved so much thirty years ago, 'All Things Great and Small', or something like that. He almost expected to see the feisty veterinarian dashing along the road beside the train in his black coupe', speeding on to his next appointment at a local farm.

When the train pulled into the Edinburgh station there were people everywhere. Unlike the trains in Germany, which pride themselves on stopping at any one station for no longer than one minute, the Scottish trains were a bit more reflective of the pace of life in this land. This was the end of the line so the locomotive shut down as soon as it backed the passenger cars into the station. There was plenty of time to gather up one's belongings and proceed to the exits.

When the O'Douls and Bryan reached the street, Timothy immediately hailed a cab. "We will be taking a taxi cab to our house," he told Bryan.

"Is there a term such as 'taxi cab' in Scotland?" Bryan asked.

"No, not really," Timothy replied. "A taxi cab is a 'hack' here," he said.

"As I recall," Bryan continued, "you have a sophisticated trolley system here in the city. I remember riding on it several years ago."

"Indeed we do," Helen responded. "In the next few days we will have plenty of opportunity to ride the trolleys to show you this ancient and wonderful town!"

When they reached the O'Doul house it was still light, and a light rain had begun. Once inside, Bryan's suitcase was placed at the bottom of the stairs and Helen took him upstairs to a small bedroom and bath. Helen and Timothy lived downstairs totally. Helen confided that Timothy had not climbed the stairs to the second floor in over ten years. "Timothy will explain all that tomorrow," she told Bryan. "We will have supper in about 30 minutes," she told Bryan. "We have cold cuts and cheese and potato salad," she said, "and a cherry pie that was made from cherries right here on our property."

Bryan thanked her for all that she had done, and then he entered the bathroom. He looked at himself in the mirror and realized that he had at least two days of beard growth. He looked for a place to plug in his electric shaver, and found none. Fortunately had had thought about this situation, and brought with him a Gillette safety razor and shaving cream. He decided to shave the next morning.

Then he made a big mistake. He took off his shoes and laid across the bed to check out the bed. It was hard but not terribly hard. The bed would do fine. That was the last thing he remembered. Soon he was fast asleep. He didn't even notice it when Helen came upstairs and covered him with a blanket. Tomorrow would be another day.

CHAPTER 3, TOURING TIME

Bryan awoke early the next morning. When he opened his eyes it was just beginning to get light outside. He had reset his wristwatch to Edinburgh time when the airplane was on final approach to Heathrow, so he knew that his watch was reflective of real time in Scotland. There wasn't a sound coming from anywhere in the house. It was 6:30 in the morning. He had slept 18 of the past 24 hours, and he didn't feel all that perky about it.

The door to the bedroom was open, and he could see a black and white cat sitting at the top of the stairs. As soon as the cat noticed that Bryan was awake, she scurried downstairs. Bryan was ready to get up, but he didn't want to make enough noise to wake up the O'Douls. So he carefully made his way to the bathroom and gently shook-up the can of shaving cream. He had not used this can in several years, so it was comforting that a white substance oozed out of the top when he bent the tip to one side on the can. Apparently canned shaving cream lasted a long time. He put a new razor blade in the Gillette razor and prepared to shave.

He was startled when he turned on the hot water and a terrible banging noise emanated from the pipes. He immediately turned off the hot water and tried the cold water. The cold water made no noise when he turned it on. It was clear that he would shave with cold water this morning.

He cut himself twice while he shaved. He knew that the cold water had nothing to do with his mis-strokes of the shaver – it was his inability to control the razor. He knew that he should have practiced with the razor while he was in Denver. "Oh well," he thought to himself, "at least I brought the styptic pencil to stop the bleeding."

Or did he? He looked everywhere in his shaving kit, but no styptic pencil was to be found. In this case there is only one thing to do – take a small piece of toilet paper and hold it against the cut until his blood clotted. Then he left the paper in place for several minutes until he was sure that the bleeding had stopped. He remembered seeing Cary Grant do this in the movie 'North by Northwest' a few years back. If it worked for Cary Grant then it ought to work for him.

So far, the noises that he had made had not awakened the O'Douls, or so he thought. About this time he heard the cat making noises downstairs and a gentle voice was speaking to the cat, advising him or her to remain silent. Bryan had lived in the clothes he was wearing for almost two days now, and it was time to find something fresh to wear. He wasn't sure what to do, but then he heard Helen coming up the stairs. "You'll have to shower downstairs," she told Bryan. "There is no hot water upstairs."

Bryan nodded in reply. "Why don't you come down and have some breakfast," she suggested, "and then you can shower afterward."

That seemed like a good idea to Bryan. He would discover as the week progressed that the O'Douls ate a hearty breakfast, usually later in the morning, and then they often skipped the noon meal completely. Helen set out one of just about every kind of breakfast that there was: eggs, ham, small pancakes, scones, and even a bagel (he could not remember any Scots who ate bagels, but food styles change with time). The scones he remembered well. These were homemade with pieces of fig in the dough. There was a butter dish in the center of the kitchen table, and three kinds of marmalade and jelly.

"We should go up and see the university today," Timothy suggested as they ate. "The school is in session most of the year, but right now they are between semesters. We could roam around and see a lot without being pestered by people handing out tracts and sales advertisements for gadgets."

"What kind of gadgets?" Bryan asked.

"Wireless telephone subscriptions mostly," Helen answered. "Every student wants a cell phone so he or she can talk all the time, while they are riding the tram or chugging up and down the hills around the university. University students always want the latest and greatest electronic gadgets in their pocketbooks, all the while complaining about the cost of higher education. For the first time in the thousand year history of the Edinburgh University, there are complaints about not enough student automobile parking at the top of the hill."

"Must be good times," Bryan suggested.

"Good times for those who are in school or who have a job," Helen said. "For the unemployed young people, times are bad."

Bryan smiled and thought about the first time he had come to Edinburgh, many years ago. He was invited to a British Army conference on armored battlefield tactics (or 'armoured' tactics, as the British spell the word). While he attended the conference, Carlie and the kids visited all the important tourist sites in the city. They had been invited to stay in the downtown flat of one of the British officers that Bryan knew at the British Army of the Rhein headquarters in Stuttgart, Germany. The officer and his family were spending the holiday at their second home, a villa in the Azores. As soon as the Wetherington family arrived, the milkman left them a note on their front door suggesting that they order milk and orange drink daily. The milk was expensive but the orange drink was free (provided by the Scottish government). Carlie decided to order milk, but declined to accept the orange drink after the kids said they didn't like it, and she left the milkman a note advising him of her decision.

The next morning, very early, there was a knock on the door. When Bryan opened the door he met the milkman, who was greatly confused. "The note that you left on the door says that you do not want the orange drink?" he asked. Yes, Bryan said, this was true – milk every day but no orange drink. "But the orange drink is free!" the milkman exclaimed. "It's free!"

Bryan explained that he understood the arrangement, but the kids had tasted the free orange drink and they just didn't like it. "Thank you, but no thank you," Bryan told the milkman. The milkman turned in total disbelief and took his quart of orange drink back down the steps with him.

Bryan also remembered the discussion he had with the landlady in the housing complex about how to ride the trolleys around the town. "When you go to the university," she suggested to Bryan, "always get off the trolley at the bottom of the hill. It costs more to ride all the way to the top. You're a young person and you can walk the hill in five minutes easily.

"How much more does it cost to ride the trolley to the top?" Bryan asked.

"Two pence," was the reply. "But it's a waste of money. You can walk it easy in five minutes." Now Bryan knew why the citizenry of Edinburgh seemed to be in such excellent health – it was the cost of the trolley rides that drove them into frequent and long walks!

The Scots have the most beautiful, lyrical flow to their speech of any group found in the modern world, and Bryan could listen all day as they spoke the king's English. But the O'Douls were not Scottish, they were Irish. The O'Douls had adopted much of the sweetness of the Scottish language, but they also kept some of the Irish lingo in their repertoire. It had taken Bryan a while to discover that the Irish of the Emerald Isle and the Scots of northern England are very different people, and they speak differently.

"Why did you all decide to settle down in Edinburgh?" Bryan asked the O'Douls. He expected to hear that the job opportunities in Scotland were better than the jobs in Ireland, but that was not the answer that Timothy gave.

"We came here because the British Military maintains an active medical program here to aid old soldiers like myself," Timothy answered. Bryan had noticed that there was a collapsible wheel chair in one corner of the living room, but so far no one had used it.

"You have medical problems?" Bryan asked.

"I have lots of medical problems," Timothy responded. Timothy was seated at the kitchen table, and he now struggled to get on his feet and step away from the chair where he was seated. He was wearing the short khaki pants made famous by the British Army in their occupation of India over a hundred years ago. When Timothy stood away from the table it was evident that he was standing on two shiny steel legs. His right leg was totally metal and his left leg was metallic to a point just below the knee. His left knee looked like the real thing, but his right knee was definitely a collection of metal castings, pulleys, and cables.

"When did all this happen?" Bryan asked.

"About a month after we parted ways in Basra," was Timothy's answer.

"You never mentioned this in any of your letters," Bryan said. "How come?"

"What did you expect?" Timothy returned. "Should I have written to you, something like: 'Hey there, Bryan Wetherington, guess what! A funny thing happened on the way to the forum today. Some not-so-friendly Iraqi blew my legs off with a rifle propelled grenade last week!'"

Bryan wasn't sure what to say, so he said nothing. "You have done a good job walking so far, so I have to conclude that you have mastered the technique of moving on two steel legs. You do a good job."

"I do a good job on the straight and level," Timothy replied. "But going up and down hills is a real problem. The press of large numbers of people around me is a terrifying experience, especially when I come up to a moving staircase, an escalator."

"You prefer elevators then?" Bryan asked.

"There are not elevators available in all the buildings," Helen responded.

"Making one's way through a crowded airport or shopping mall is a team effort," Timothy said. "If we reach an escalator, Helen always moves close to me on my left side and we take the first step to get on the escalator together. My left leg is far more maneuverable than my right, so I always take important steps with my left leg."

"We have had fourteen years to work all this out," Timothy added.

"If we are going somewhere where the terrain is hilly or irregular, we can always take the wheelchair," Helen added. "But we tend to avoid those situations."

"Can both of you drive your car?" Bryan asked.

"Helen does all the driving for this family," Timothy responded. "Of course, we drive very little. Gasoline is over $6.00 a gallon, American. But we live only one block from the tram stop, and that is our window to the world."

"We don't visit our family very often," Helen added. "Mostly, they come here to see us. We go to London every other year or so to see our son, Nygel, and his family. He drives a delivery truck for a medical company, and the work has been good for him. They have three children."

"You also have a daughter living in Manchester," Bryan noted.

"Yes," Helen answered. "Her name is Caroline. She and her family come to see us much more often than Nygel's family because they are so much closer to Edinburgh. She is a Public Health Nurse. It helps to have a member in the family who understands medicines. All medicines are free here, but it is a bit of a problem to make sure Timothy receives the right medicines."

"You Yanks have to wait until you are age 65 to receive free medicines, don't you?" Timothy asked.

"Not if you are a retired military person," Bryan answered. "But, other than a one-a-day pill for high blood pressure, I don't take any pills."

"There are no pills for hearing problems, are there?" Timothy asked.

Bryan laughed. "So you noticed," he told the O'Douls. "I don't hear very well. I think it all started in the cupola of an Abrams tank, and I was never able to regain my hearing in my right ear."

"Does your government aid you with your hearing problems?" Helen asked.

"Not really," Bryan responded. "So long as you have some hearing in one ear, the Veteran's Administration won't contribute to the purchase of hearing aids and things like that. When my right ear quit completely about five years ago I got a device imbedded in my skull that transfers all the sounds on my right side to my good ear on the left side, and it seems to work pretty well."

"Uncle Sam paid for that?" Timothy asked.

"No, I paid for that," Bryan responded. "It cost me five grand. But I do draw a retirement check from the Army every month, and for that I am thankful."

"Do you have a balance problem?" Helen asked. "I noticed last night that you held rather tightly to the handrails of the escalator when we were dashing to the train."

"Yes, I have a balance problem," Bryan confessed.

"Then we are truly brothers in more ways than we knew!" Timothy said. "But we can still see with our eyes, we can feel what's around us, and we can go places without a lot of intensive preparation. A few months ago we got an invitation to travel to Manchester to the den where the Beatles got their start, and Paul McCartney sang for us. People treat us pretty well."

"Timothy even has his own private booth at the pub next to the tram," Helen explained. "A lot of people use the booth, but the owner always clears it out when Timothy and I come for fish and chips."

"We always go there on Thursday nights, so he has a pretty good idea when we are coming," Timothy added. "He has this huge TV set and we watch soccer. You haven't seen outstanding soccer until you have seen the Manchester Guardians."

"Most people don't know this," Timothy added, "but that pub owner has never charged Helen or myself for the first pint of beer since we walked into that place. We pay for food, but never the drink. The first time we rolled into the pub I was in a wheelchair, and we got a standing wave of applause from the customers."

"So Scotsmen support the war effort in the Middle East?" Bryan asked.

"I think they support the Scottish regiments who have been doing the Crown's dirty work for the past four hundred years," Timothy replied. "Unemployment has always been a problem in the northern UK, and many young people think of the military as a haven to get away from home and start a life."

"Did your son ever go into the service?" Bryan asked.

Helen answered quickly. "No, he never had a desire to do that. He was 23 years old when Timothy was airlifted from Qatar to the Army hospital in Manchester, and he understood fully the game of roulette that one plays when one joins the Army."

"Are any of your children in the military?" Helen asked.

"No," Bryan replied. "All three of them found other ways to make a life, and to be honest, Carlie and I were glad that they did."

There had been no mention of the agenda for the day, and Bryan was afraid to ask because he wasn't sure what the limits were on Timothy's travels. Helen must have recognized his dilemma so she filled him in on the plan for the day. "Timothy mentioned last night that we could visit the University, but we can change all that. We could visit the downtown today and have lunch at Pierson's Restaurant on the city square. It's one of the oldest restaurants in town, and they serve a delicious noon meal."

That would be fine with Bryan.

"We bought this house for several reasons," Timothy offered. "First of all, it is only one block from the tram and the path from the house to the tram is flat. There is a concrete footpath all the way to the tram. This house has one bedroom on the main floor, and we needed that. But the thing I liked the best about this house is that it has a dishwasher in the kitchen and the clothes washer is on the back porch. About a year after we bought this house, our kids bought us a clothes dryer so Helen doesn't have to hang clothes out in the back yard any more."

"Have you ever seen the TV series 'All in the Family'?" Helen asked.

Oh yes, Bryan knew all about that series. He knew all about Archie Bunker and Edith, and their son-in-law, Meathead, and their daughter.

"Well, that series really started here in England, under the name of 'Married, with Children'," Helen said. "Norman Lear took it to the States and it was popular beyond anything that we had ever seen before. We bought the largest TV set that we could place next to our fireplace in the living room and one of the furniture stores close to the tram sold us two 'Archie' and 'Edith' reclining chairs just like the Bunker family had. They sold the recliners to us at less than half price."

Bryan looked into the living room and saw the TV set that was the center of attraction. The recliners were leather, and they were well-worn.

"Can you get the soccer games here?" Bryan asked.

"Oh yes, oh yes," Timothy replied. "But it's much better to watch the Guardians on the big TV at the pub. The people around add a lot to the show."

ᏉᎤ   ᏉᎤ   ᏉᎤ

As the trio was making their way to the tram station, Helen began to speak about her job at a local dry cleaning company. The company was about five miles away, but it was located on the same trolley line as the one they were walking toward right now. "I really enjoy my job," she told Bryan. "I was an entry-level bookkeeper when Timothy and I met in Manchester many, many years ago, and everywhere we went I always managed to find part-time work at some business establishment. Our kids never seemed to mind spending a part of their day in a nursery school or something like that when I went to work. Caroline swears to this day that the time she spent in the nursery school when she was four years old was the happiest time of her life. She is a very outgoing person, and attending a nursery school was right up her alley."

Bryan and Carlie had encountered the same sort of situation when they were young, and Bryan remembered it well. Carlie liked to work in the school system, and the hours she spent there were about the same hours that the kids spent in their school work. "The kids grew up in a hurry," Bryan mentioned. "I was separated from the family during the Persian Gulf conflict and then again during the Bosnian debacle, but other than that I worked a nine-to-five job in America or in Europe. The kids seemed to enjoy living in Europe, but we knew that we had to get them back to the States before they lost all traces of an American 'psyche'. We spent most of our stateside time at Fort Hood, near Kileen, Texas. That area of Texas is pretty much semi-desert, but it doesn't get so cold in the winter that the kids are forced indoors. Our kids knew that there was a big climate difference between central Europe and western Texas, but they didn't seem to prefer one over the other."

"You spent a lot of time in Vietnam, didn't you?" Timothy asked.

"I spent two tours there," Bryan replied. "I was an artilleryman in those days, and it wasn't until Carlie and I were married and spent time in the States that I was able to transfer to the armored."

"Do you mind talking about Vietnam?" Timothy asked.

"Oh no, not at all," Bryan replied.

"Well, the reason I ask is this," Timothy responded. "Vietnam is the only war that the United Kingdom declined to join in with you Yanks, and for the first time in history we watched the whole show from the bleachers. I would like to hear how you feel about that war."

Helen had the perfect solution. "We can eat supper early and talk in the living room. This will be a perfect night to talk shop because the Guardians are not playing."

CHAPTER 4, VIETNAM

On the way back from the trolley-tour of downtown Edinburgh, the trio stopped at a large grocery store close to the tram stop and they wandered through the delicatessen section where there were all kinds of prepared foods to catch the eye of the hungry buyer. Helen insisted that she was not a very good cook, which Bryan took to mean that she had spent most of her adult life working outside of the home and baking cookies for the children and cooking four-course meals for each evening meal was out of the question. Timothy insisted that he did his part of the cooking also. Apparently the two of them made a trip to the Army Commissary on the outskirts of Edinburgh about once a month and they bought the bulk of the food that they would consume in the next month. This was the longest trip that they would make in their car for the entire month.

Timothy pointed out where he and Helen attended church on 'some' Sundays – an Anglican Church that looked several hundred years old. Later, Helen confided that they had not been to church for a regular Sunday service in over two years, but that was because Timothy was usually not up to making the drive early on a Sunday morning. "If we go to the early service," Helen explained, "we have to drive in a bit of a morning rush. And if we go to the later service then Timothy might miss a part of the Guardians game." It was a tough decision to make.

"I get very nervous when we drive in heavy traffic," Helen admitted.

After the evening dishes were placed in the dishwasher and Helen raised some semi-classical music on their stereo set, the trio sat down in the living room to talk. Helen was careful to offer 'her' recliner to Bryan, but he insisted on sitting on the sofa.

"Do you prefer tea or coffee?" Helen asked.

"Either one would be fine," was Bryan answer. "Which do you drink in the evenings?" he asked.

The O'Douls looked at each other. "I like the decaf coffee," Timothy responded, "but Helen prefers some of the stronger British teas. We make coffee one night, and then tea the next."

"Is this a coffee night or a tea night?" Bryan asked.

"Definitely a 'tea' night," Timothy responded. "If you don't mind, we'll sip a bit of tea in honor of the Queen mother, who passed away not too long ago."

"She lived a long and memorable life," Bryan said.

"And her daughter will do the same," Helen suggested. "For someone who has had the entire English world at her disposal for the past fifty years, Queen Elizabeth II looks pretty good!"

"I'll drink to that," Bryan responded.

While Helen was making the tea, Timothy raised himself out of his recliner and walked over to a writing desk next to the front door. He began searching for something in the desk, and Helen came to his rescue when the water began to boil. "I cut this article out of the London newspaper last week," Timothy told Bryan, "when I knew that you were coming to visit. It's a long article about the cost of the Vietnam War, comparing it with what the UK and the USA have spent on the ongoing Iraqi war."

"You have access to the London newspapers?" Bryan asked.

"We can buy the Sunday paper up here in Edinburgh," Timothy replied, "but not the dailys. I wouldn't want to read the London paper every day anyway. Our local daily newspaper does a pretty good job of local and international news."

"Do the London newspapers treat the Prime Minister kindly?" Bryan asked.

"They pounce on him every chance they get!" was the reply. "Somewhere between 70 and 80 percent of the English people want *out* of Iraq right now, but the Prime Minister keeps sticking with the Yanks. The big question that most Brits are asking is this: 'What does

Tony Blair seek to gain by keeping our troops in Iraq? No one seems to know the answer."

Helen entered the room with a large tray. The tray contained a large tea pot, three large tea cups on saucers, a supply of milk, and a sugar bowl. "We don't use sugar cubes in this house," Helen said, "because Timothy always ends up using two and a half or three and a half cubes."

"Regular sugar will be fine," Bryan responded. He was surprised at the size of the tea cups – they were huge. "Whenever we see Miss Marple on Public Television she is always drinking from a tiny tea cup. Your tea cups are significantly larger," Bryan said.

"Miss Marple always drinks afternoon tea, which is taken in small cups. The evening tea is served in much larger cups so one does not have to refill the cups so frequently," Helen replied.

Both Timothy and Helen gave up on finding the Vietnam War article in the writing desk. "I can remember most of what it said," Timothy suggested.

Everyone prepared their tea, sipped upon it for a moment, and then Timothy opened the evening's discussion with "Tell us all about Vietnam, Bryan."

Since Bryan had been warned earlier in their correspondence that this conversation was going to occur, he felt like he was well prepared. "When I joined the U. S. Army in 1965 I had just graduated from high school. I was single and didn't have any special girlfriend. I drove over to Ft. Stewart, Georgia and filled out the paperwork. Since the draft was on, I could either volunteer immediately for the draft or I could 'join' the Army as a volunteer. A person so drafted served two years and a volunteer served three years. The enlistment Sergeant explained that I was way ahead of the game to 'volunteer' because I would have my choice of assignment. As a draftee I would have no such choices."

"So I volunteered, signed up to enter the service immediately, and was offered a slot in either the infantry, armored, or artillery. For some reason I picked the 'artillery', but to this day I don't know why I did that. For sure I didn't want to be in the infantry, and I wasn't exactly sure what the people in the 'armored' did. Anyway, I was off to basic training a month later, and then reported to Fort Sill, Oklahoma to learn how to shoot large caliber weapons. After basic artillery I went through an advanced artillery course and got my orders to report to the 173rd Airborne Brigade in Okinawa. Someone figured out that I didn't know how to jump out of an airplane, so they sent me to Fort Benning to become a jumper. I didn't want to become a 'jumper', but it was too late to back out now. So I finished airborne training, returned to Fort Sill, declined any sort of Ranger training, and was on my way to Okinawa by early 1966."

"A Marine Division had already been sent to a place called 'Da Nang' so we knew that America was in this Vietnam War for real now. What I did not know was that the 173rd was already packing up for a transfer to Vietnam also, and shortly after I arrived in Okinawa I found myself on an airplane headed for the hills just north of Saigon in the Long Khan Province. We were stationed at lots of places, like Cam Ranh Bay, etc. We were trained in firing the 105mm Howitzer, but once we arrived in Vietnam we took off all the armament on the howitzer so it could be transported by an H-47 twin-rotor helicopter. One helicopter transported the howitzer and a second helicopter carried our ammunition in a huge hemp net below the chopper."

"We did okay in Vietnam, but on a couple of occasions we found ourselves left high and dry on the backside of some hill when the VC found out that we were there and we had no way to leave. Once our helicopters left, our means of escape left also."

"We supported lots of different units, like the 25th Infantry Division and the 1st Marine Division, but we mostly stayed with the 173rd Airborne Brigade."

"Did you ever get to see Saigon?" Timothy asked.

"Oh yes," Bryan replied. "Every guy in my outfit lived for the days he would be dumped into the back of a five-ton ammunition truck and transported to Saigon for a weekend of drinking, women, and general debauchery. Every time it came close to getting a 'three day pass' the unit would be gathered into one place for a sermon by the brigade chaplain. He would warn us of the evils that we might find in Saigon – the women who carried every venereal disease known to man (and then some), the cheap liquor, and worst of all, the drugs that every GI could buy on every street corner in Saigon that might send you into the next world before your time. The Chaplain wasn't all that convincing, but he was always followed by our First Sergeant, who had a series of slides that he liked to show to his young troopers."

"The first few slides were of GIs with their pants and shorts removed, showing what was left of their penises and scrotums. Some of the guys had penises that looked like leafy broccoli sprouts, and the color was green. These were guys who had contracted some venereal diseases known only in the Pacific rim, and the Army Medical Corps was still trying to figure out how to heal them. The First Sergeant kept harping on the fact that a little penicillin wasn't going to heal the venereal infection that these guys had."

"Then he would finish up his show with pictures of GIs who were hooked on various drugs. Some of them didn't look all that bad, unless he showed a close-up picture where you could see the GI's eyes. These guys couldn't focus on *anything*. We were reminded that both the venereal disease cases and the drug cases were shipped back to Fort Lewis in Washington State and put in some hospital to see if they could be patched-up well enough to be sent home. The Army didn't want America to know what bad shape some of these soldiers were in."

"So there we were, in the back of our five-ton ammo truck, dressed in civilian clothes, all the money that we had saved for several months in our pockets, and a package of a dozen condoms in our billfolds, anxiously awaiting the liftoff of the truck to Saigon! It was quite an experience."

The O'Douls made no statement. Helen got up and offered more tea to everyone.

"There is something else I should add," Bryan said. "Every GI who returned from Saigon was passed through the medical services tent and given a lot of shots to ward off some of the evils that the Chaplain and the First Sergeant talked about. There was a new type of penicillin available every few months, and the Army was the biggest user of the medicines."

"You stayed there one year?" Timothy asked.

"Yes, exactly one year," Bryan responded. "The President hadn't decided to extend the GI's enlistments in Vietnam when I was there. It was a few years later before the soldiers found out that they had to remain in Vietnam longer than they originally planned because there were no replacements for them coming from the States."

"The same thing is happening in Iraq right now, to both the Yanks and the Brits," Timothy added.

"What happened when you rotated back to the States?" Timothy asked.

"I left Vietnam the first time as a Sergeant E5," Bryan answered. "I flew to Fort Lewis, the entry point to the United States, passed my urine test, and was returned to Fort Sill. It took a couple of days for me to clear the 'debarkation point' in Washington State because a big scandal had broken out. Some of the medics were selling their 'pure' urine for about $25 a vial to the returning GIs who weren't so sure that they could pass the urine test. If you flunked the test you might not get home for a couple of months."

"I had sixty days of leave coming, so I returned to South Georgia to relax. According to my enlistment papers, I had a full year guaranteed in the States before the Army could ship me back to Vietnam, and I counted on that. I was kind of sweet on one of the girls that I graduated from high school with two years earlier, and I corresponded with her the whole time I was in Vietnam. So we got together and got married about a month after I returned from Vietnam."

"You're talking about Carlie?" Timothy asked.

"Yes, Carlie Stevens," Bryan answered. "She was the prettiest gal I ever met, and she seemed to be interested in me too, so getting married was easy. We had known each other for five or six years by then, so this was no whirlwind romance."

Helen seemed to be a little more comfortable with the conversation now. "Did you have an option *not* to return to Vietnam after a year?" Helen asked.

"No, not really," Bryan responded. "My enlistment was for three years and I would be eligible to return with six months left on my enlistment. The Army had me right where they wanted me --- I was going back to Vietnam as soon as possible."

"What did you do the second time you went to Vietnam?" Timothy asked.

"Strangely enough," Bryan responded, "I ended up in the same 173rd Airborne Brigade that I started out with two years earlier. But the Brigade was now assigned to the 'Vietnamization' program farther to the south, mostly in the Mekong Delta, so that was where I ended up. We didn't fight nearly as much on my second tour, but we never stopped looking over our shoulder because there was always the threat of sudden violence."

"Why sudden violence?" Helen asked.

"Because you never knew if the person walking toward you was a simple farmer going from one rice paddy to another, or a Viet Cong armed with a fragmentation grenade that he would throw at you as soon as you passed. The good guys and the bad guys all looked alike there."

Bryan continued with, "It really got tense when the rice crop was ready for harvest. The VC would come out of the hills around the rice paddies to take away 'their share' of the crop to feed themselves. I guess the farmers didn't have any choice but to give them what they wanted."

There was a long pause. "When I read about the final evacuation of the South Vietnamese government and all the Americans in Saigon in 1975," Bryan continued, "the TV stories about people hanging onto helicopters at the U. S. Embassy, trying to get out of Saigon any way they could, I couldn't help but think of one thing in the Mekong Delta. I thought about the farmer who had been forced to give food to some smartass Viet Cong for about twenty years, a VC who never did the first lick of work in those rice paddies and yet he came there to 'share' the crop every summer. Well, after 1975 some of those VC probably showed up just like they always had before, but this time there was no reason for any farmer to give them anything. In my mind's eye I can see some farmer who had collected a few weapons of his own, maybe a Russian AK-47 assault rifle with a small amount of ammunition, waiting patiently for the VC to come and demand their tribute. The farmer might even greet the VC when he came into their home, and invite him to drink a glass of that terrible ale that the farmers concocted from fermented rice, before he led him out to the barn to pick up the food and shoot him in the back. There was plenty of room to bury a human being in those rice paddies, and the body would make good fertilizer for the next growing season."

Bryan continued with, "You know, in America and in England, any time there is a military draft that has been voted into law by a Congress or a Parliament, parents look at their fifteen or sixteen year old sons and pray that the event that forced the draft will end quickly. Can you imagine how it must have been in those rice paddies when the VC would come down out of the hills every summer and demand not only food, but people-support in some cases. They would have the farmer package the rice for transport to the north, then demand that the farmer provide a strong back to 'carry the food some part of the way' to the north. The VC would pick out the largest young male in the family and demand that he assist them in getting the rice to some collection point. After the VC left, the family would hope and pray that the kid who was carrying the food would be allowed to return the next day. If he didn't return in a day or two, the farmer had to assume that his kid was now a member of the VC, and he may never see him again."

"What you have just said is another page in the living document named 'War Is Hell'," Timothy suggested. "Just about the time we think that things are as bad as they can get, we discover that there are people on this earth who are planning the next rape of the poor and the meek."

"One thing is for sure," Bryan added, "the term 'Domino Theory' shall forever be banned from the Department of Defense lingo. Everyone in the Pentagon spoke about how the Communists would overrun all of Asia unless we Americans held our ground in Vietnam. Those people always forgot to mention that the French had tried to 'hold their ground' for a generation in that same country, and failed. Yet the whole time that this war was going on, no one bothered to talk to Ho Chi Minh and find out what his vision of Vietnam was. I have serious doubts that he was ever a Communist. He was a 'Vietnam for the Vietnamese' person, and we refused to accept that."

"At least your former Secretary of Defense, Mr. MacNamera, was willing to publicly acknowledge his mistakes a generation or so after the war," Helen said. "Very few politicians ever do that."

"Which points out that Mr. MacNamera was really a strategic planner, never a politician," Bryan suggested.

It was time to turn in for the evening. Helen cleared away the dishes and put them in the dishwasher. "Do you like to take showers in the evening or the morning?" Timothy asked.

"I prefer the evenings," Bryan answered. "I don't like to feel sweaty when I go to sleep."

"Then you ought to take a shower now," Timothy suggested. "I am also an evening shower person, and Helen likes a morning shower."

"I will be careful not to use up the hot water," Bryan said.

"You sound like a person who comes from a large family," Timothy suggested.

"No, not large," Bryan responded, "but I soon learned that teenagers just keep running the shower water until the hot water runs out completely. All my kids used to shower in the morning so I always showered at night."

Helen came back into the living room. "What's on tap tomorrow?" she asked.

Timothy looked at her and she looked at both of them. "We have an opportunity tomorrow that we cannot pass up," she said. "Caroline has offered to take the three of us to Manchester tomorrow to see a real soccer game between the Manchester Guardians and one of the other league teams. She guarantees that the seats are good – according to her *all* the seats in the arena are good.

This was not Bryan's call to make. "Timothy," he asked, "are you up to wrestling with a soccer crowd tomorrow?"

Timothy didn't hesitate for a second. "Bring 'em on," he said. "Tell Caroline that we accept her invitation."

"We will have to spend the night in Manchester," Helen cautioned.

"Does Caroline have room for three adults in her flat?" Timothy asked.

"Yes, she does," Helen answered. "She sends the kids down the street to one of the neighbors and we can sleep in the kids' beds."

Bryan raised his hand quickly. "Tell Caroline to find us two motel rooms close by, something on the first floor, and I will pay for the rooms. It's the least I can do while I am here."

Helen was pleased with the suggestion. "I will call her and make the arrangements early tomorrow morning," she said.

"Do you really want to continue to shave with that old Gillette razor?" Timothy asked. "You can use my electric, and save a lot of face that way."

Bryan liked the idea. "Good idea," he said. "I'll use a real English electric razor tomorrow!"

CHAPTER 5, THE GUARDIANS

Caroline arrived early the next morning in her car, which looked a great deal like the Chrysler PT runabout that Bryan saw all over the States. It was definitely a four-passenger car, no more. Caroline's mission was to get the trio to the soccer arena by 2 o'clock in the afternoon, and there was plenty of time for that.

"I called the motel early this morning before I left town, and they assured me that would provide transportation for us to the game from the motel, which is only three blocks from the arena. When I mentioned that my father was a wheelchair patient they told me that they would make the special arrangements to put him on the lift at the back of the arena and set him up at a special observation deck just below the press windows. He will have one of the best seats in the house and the two of you will sit slightly below him. All the seats on that special platform are portable – you can set them anywhere you want."

"You're not going to the game?" Bryan asked.

"Oh no, not me," was Caroline's reply. "I get my fill of the Manchester Guardians on local TV. Beside, I was lucky to get the three tickets."

On the way to Manchester, driving on the M-6 freeway, Timothy asked some questions about the medical people who sold their urine to soldiers returning from Vietnam during the war. "Did the government ever straighten that out?" he asked Bryan.

"I suppose so," was the answer. "Anyway, the story went away after a while. Americans can only concentrate on one story like that for two or three days maximum, and then they flip the TV dial or the newspaper page to find something else to see or read."

"The English newspapers reported for many days about the fact that your President made such careful preparation to become a pilot during the Vietnam era, and then failed to show up for a simple flight physical. A lot of people want to know what happened that day," Timothy said.

"We will never know," Bryan answered. "All the official records of all the events that occurred before, during, and after that episode in the Air National Guard have been 'expunged' from the archives of the federal government. The first President Bush made sure of that."

"So there is no explanation of why the second Mr. Bush failed to show up for his flight physical?" Carolina asked.

"So far as I know," Bryan answered. "Some of the tabloids have hinted at the fact that the Air Force had a new test that prospective pilots were forced to take at that time that would show the presence of many types of drugs in one's blood. They speculate that Bush #2 knew better than to subject himself to such a test at that time."

"I guess if you know that you are going to fail a medical test and it is important that you do *not* fail the test, one way to step around the problem is to not show up," Timothy suggested.

"We will never know the truth about what happened that day, and why," Bryan said. "End of story."

"I don't think our Prime Minister, Mr. Blair, has any skeletons like that in his closet," Caroline mentioned. "People are angry at him for keeping UK troops in Iraq, but on a personal basis he seems to be a virtuous person. It's hard to become truly angry with Mr. Blair, unless of course, you are one of the unfortunate families that lost a son or daughter in Iraq."

"There are lots of families in America who have lost sons and daughters in Iraq and Afghanistan," Bryan responded. "And no one seems to know what to do about it. One thing is for sure: The President of the United States is very much a captive in his 'White House World' on Pennsylvania Avenue, and he cannot stray away from that location without significant preparation on the part of security people."

Bryan continued with, "I wonder if Mr. Blair feels the same pressure to remain in his own private 'green zone' in London?"

"I don't think so," Helen responded. "He is a consummate public speaker, and he will not pass up an opportunity to address the UK family."

Then Helen added, "The one I worry about is the Queen. She may have a lot of security people clustered about her, but that is not evident whenever she appears on the TV. And she appears on the TV almost every day of her life."

"Without appearing to be a cynic," Caroline suggested, "I wonder if the Queen misses Princess Diane every now and then. When Diane was alive she kept the newspapers and television busy covering every facet of her life, and the Queen was left alone. Elizabeth II may have been a little angry with her daughter-in-law, but Diane also served a lot of useful purposes."

Everyone agreed.

The group arrived at the motel an hour before the game began and the owner of the motel moved swiftly to deliver Timothy O'Doul to the base of the lift at the arena. "There is a young man who will meet you at the arena and he will remain with you until the game is over and you are safely back in the minivan," the proprietor told Timothy. "Every now and then the crowd gets a little rowdy and we don't want anything bad to happen to you, you being a Persian Gulf Hero and all that."

Timothy looked straight into the eyes of the proprietor, thanked him for the special efforts that he was making to deliver them to the big soccer game, and then ended the conversation with the comment, "the fact that a person loses his legs in combat does not necessarily mean that he is a Hero, Sir. It is possible that he may be just a totally inept soldier, and that is all."

Surprisingly the proprietor agree with him: "I know that, Sir," he said, "but we like to give our soldiers the benefit of the doubt."

ᔥ   ᔥ   ᔥ

This exciting day did not end with only a victory for the Manchester Guardians before a sellout crowd at the soccer arena. The Guardians got that, and then the O'Doul party was invited upstairs to meet some of the players and attend a smorgasbord put on by management. As they made their way back to the motel, Bryan was pleased that he had suggested the motel arrangement because it was already dark, and any trip all the way back to Edinburgh at this time of day would be agony for everyone in the car. Caroline promised to pick them up in front of the motel at nine o'clock the next morning.

Bryan assumed that Timothy would be the first person to 'fade' completely after this big day of sporting events, etc., but it was Helen who showed the affects of the long day first. Timothy asked Bryan if he could spend some time in Bryan's room while Helen prepared for bed, and Bryan quickly agreed. "I snore so badly that it is difficult for Helen to fall asleep when she has had a tiring day," Timothy admitted. "She needs a little time by herself, and then I will join her."

"I am told that there are devices that minimize one's snoring," Bryan mentioned. "It may not be long before I have to get one of them because I also have a snoring problem at times. Carlie has not suggested that I purchase such a thing, but like I say, it's time may be at hand soon."

"When we get back to Edinburgh I will show you my 'sleeping kit'," Timothy said. "When you first get it, it is hard to sleep with a mask over the front of your face, but your face finally accepts that limitation. I will show it to you tomorrow evening when we are back at our house."

Bryan nodded in agreement.

"Where did you find out about this sleeping kit?" Bryan asked.

"My son gave it to me on Fathers' Day a couple of years ago. I think he has one that he uses, and both father and son have the same impediments. It's all in the genes, you know."

Timothy continued with, "When I read about the deaths and the severe injuries that some of our GIs are encountering in Iraq and Afghanistan, I always think about how young some of these men are, and how the rest of their lives are all screwed up. A man my age (and I will soon be 58 years old) learns to expect a certain amount of limitation in one's activities and a commensurate amount of pain to accompany every false move. But how do you explain that to a twenty-year-old who had suddenly lost partial or complete use of his arms or legs, or eyesight?"

"I'm not saying that it would have been better if these men had died on the battlefield, but I know of no possible way to extend to them heartfelt assurance that they will have a better life later. I have never considered taking my own life because of my legless situation, but compared to some of the men returning from Iraq and Afghanistan today, I am a simple case. I know that I can walk from here to the tram, eat, drink, and be merry, but some of those young people can't even count on that."

There was a long pause. "One thing is for sure," Timothy continued. "When you come home from war in little pieces, your sex life suffers interminably."

Bryan agreed with Timothy's statement, and he was not one of the men who was severely injured in battle. He had lost most of his hearing, and that was all. "I would imagine that what you are saying is correct," Bryan returned, "even though I have never suffered personally like you have because of the gods of war. I do know, that injured or not, we lose our sexual drives in leaps and bounds as we get older. Sex is a two-way street, and we all want to be sexually aroused by our partner while we support our spouses in their sexual needs. I do know that it is becoming increasingly difficult for me to hold an erection for any long period of time – long enough to allow Carlie to reach some level of orgasm."

"The medical journals say that there are new drugs coming out on the market that will help us old guys maintain an erection, and I applaud that," Timothy said. "But there is another aspect to having successful sex, and that is keeping the nerve endings in your penis 'alive' so you can feel something good happening when you are having sex. I haven't read anything about implanting new nerve endings in one's male organ to send happy signals back to the brain during sex."

"The truth is, doctors could probably implant such devices, but they wouldn't know where to hook them up to," Bryan suggested.

"No one has ever had the courage to ask me how a person like me has sex," Timothy mentioned. "When I was a kid and the 'thalidomide' scare raced around the world, we had a magistrate in our local court who had no arms. He wrote everything with a pencil between his teeth, and he was an excellent judge. But every time his name came up in conversation (especially after the group had had a few drinks), someone broached the subject of how an armless man can wipe his own ass after he defecates. That was always an interesting discussion, but I would imagine that no one in the precinct ever asked the judge personally about this question."

The men laughed. "In my case," Timothy continued, "I will tell you that I remove all this paraphernalia when its beddy-bye time. My left leg is simply a stump, and the new lower leg and foot that was given to me here in Edinburgh slips off easily. The leg needs this time out of the 'socket' so the skin can grow and any abrasions can heal. But my right leg is missing all the way past the knee, and that presents a new set of problems."

"Are you sure you want to talk about all this?" Bryan asked.

"Absolutely," Timothy responded quickly. "I get a new right leg about every two years or so, and it represents the best designs of a group of technicians and doctors who are spending their entire adult lives trying to make better prosthetics. A few of the techies at the Army clinic actually wear prosthetic devices themselves because they have been wounded in battle. Some surgeons have figured out a way to attach a cable to the end of a muscle in the upper leg, and that new cable is the start of a whole new way of life. They tell me that the knee joint would have been easy to replicate if it didn't have to roll left or right in the socket. They use the terms 'pitch' and 'yaw' for the knee movements, just like the designers of fighter aircraft do. One does not 'roll' one's lower bones (where the tibia and fibula used to be), but one 'pitches' and 'yaws' the new structure to replicate the old bones. If I insisted on running in an Olympic race then the technicians would probably have to become more creative in their designs, but all I want is to be able to make it from the house to the tram station or get down an escalator at the shopping mall."

"Do you keep the right leg intact when you go to bed?" Bryan asked.

"No, not really," was the answer. "I can disconnect the cables from the prosthesis, which allows my muscles to relax. And I can also remove the leg from my upper thigh. At that point I need have no fear that something in the pulley, cable, and leg structure will catch in the bedsheets and damage my torso. The problem is, once my legs have been removed, I have no lower-limb mobility. I am reduced to movement on the bed by lifting myself with my arms only."

Bryan was hoping that this discussion was over, but Timothy had more to say. "I usually sleep pretty good once I am settled in bed. I can roll either to my left or right, but my body soon returns to its preferred position, which is sleeping on my back. I insert the catheter in the end of my penis so I won't wet the bed because it is too difficult to get up during the night to go to the bathroom. On those infrequent nights when Helen and I decide to have sex, we are faced with a decision: whether it is better for me to be on the 'bottom', where Helen does most of the work, or to try to maintain a spot on the top, which is difficult for me. I suspect that as time passes I will find it too difficult to be on top, and I will become a permanent bottom person the rest of my life."

The TV was burbling forth with something, but the two men in the room sat silently for a time. "What you have described," Bryan said, "is a decision that just about every couple in the world will have to face sooner or later. You two have faced the problem quite early, but I am sure that Carlie and I will have a similar problem in the next ten years or so. The gods of fertility do not endow their subjects with unending sexual pleasures, no matter what they do."

"Maybe God didn't intend for people to carry on like that after they pass some intermediate age, like 55 or so," Timothy suggested.

"It could be, it could be," Bryan agreed. "Anyway, I find that Carlie is an extremely pleasant person to sleep with, even if the extent of our interaction on a particular night is only touching one-another."

"I agree wholeheartedly," Timothy responded. "I have suggested on a couple of occasions that Helen and I should sleep in different rooms, mostly because of the way I snore. But she insists that she will not sleep alone. I think she was the mover behind our son's 'sleeping kit' gift on Fathers' Day, and I appreciate it also. She says that when she reaches out in the middle of the night she wants to feel me there, close by, breathing and sweating. After all, we only have each other now. And I must admit that I get a great sexual lift just seeing her coming out of the shower, dripping wet, with shiny breasts and tiny thighs and legs. She is a beauty to behold! She probably hasn't gained over twenty pounds in the thirty-plus years we have been married, and she looks absolutely ravishing when she leaves the house in the morning for work. I tell her how great she looks a lot, but she never seems to be sure whether or not I mean it."

Again, a pause in the action.

"When you were talking about Vietnam last night," Timothy began, "you mentioned about the 'three day passes' to Saigon and the prostitution and drugs in the city. You never said how you got around that. Since we are having such a frank discussion tonight, do you care to elaborate a bit about those revolting days?"

Bryan had to laugh. "Well, to be honest, after I saw the pictures that the First Sergeant showed constantly of men my age with green, split-end penises and cloudy eyes that made them look like worn-out old men, I tried to stay away from the bars and bordellos in Saigon. But every young man who is past puberty builds up quantities of semen that cry for a way out of the body, and whether it be the 'wet dreams' of a thirteen year old in his bed at night or a young soldier trying to sleep in a private space in a rice paddy, the young man will always unzip his pants and masturbate with glee. There is no disease transferred, no drugs kill his mind, but there is a peace that follows as his mind generates thoughts of full-breasted naked women running before him in the night. Sometimes his body jerks wildly in the replication of a sexual orgy. The semen is sticky and will mess up his trousers, so he has to find a way to place the residue in a cup or wipe it on a piece of paper that can be left in the nearby brush. That was my way of making it through Vietnam twice."

"We British participate in those kinds of activities also," Timothy admitted. "Wherever we were, be it in the Falklands or Belize or Cyprus or Bosnia or Kosovo or Iraq, my greatest fear was that some group of our young British GIs would come upon a young woman who looked sexually desirable to them and seemed very willing to participate in their fantasies. There was no telling what would happen next. It didn't seem to matter what the women were wearing, or what their religious background was. They were candidates for rape and unspeakable molestation, and those of us in the front office were helpless to stop it."

"This is yet another chapter in the ongoing saga, 'War is Hell in Many Ways.'" Both men nodded in agreement. "We will see you for breakfast in the lobby tomorrow morning," Timothy reminded Bryan.

"The breakfast is free, so we shouldn't miss it. Let's go to the lobby at 8 a.m."

CHAPTER 6, MATTERS SPIRITUAL

The next morning, Caroline took the trio on a whirlwind tour of the city of Manchester while the church bells rang merrily, and then she headed north on M-6 toward Edinburgh. She asked Bryan if he wanted to make a side trip to Stratford-on-Avon and view the Shakespearean theatre and the Ann Hathaway cottage there, but Bryan had seen all of this before. Beside, all of this was south of Manchester and the trio wanted to return to the north.

A lively discussion about Mr. Shakespeare ensued as they motored along the freeway. "I think I came to a much better appreciation of Shakespeare after I watched the movie, 'Shakespeare in Love' a few years ago," Bryan began, "even though I knew that everything in that movie was a bunch of baloney. Nevertheless, it made the Bard more of a person to me than ever before."

"The London critics blasted the movie intensely, saying that there was no evidence that Anne Hathaway spent all of her days in Stratford alone while husband William caroused in London for half of a lifetime," Caroline asserted.

"It was still a funny story," Helen suggested, "especially the parts with the Queen. I think the actress who played the Queen stole the show!"

Everyone agreed.

"I hope that all these idiotic searches through ancient tombs and catacombs by persons hoping to prove that William Shakespeare really did not write most of the plays ceases and desists," Timothy said. "You have to wonder what the motivation of these 'non-believers' is."

"One thing is for sure," Bryan added. "Mr. Shakespeare's plays will continue to be seen on the world's stage for centuries to come, and in fact, they may eventually be translated into all modern languages so the world can laugh and cry at the English pranks that he wrote about."

"I would guess that he described people the way that they actually lived, and the audience appreciates that," Helen added.

Hear, hear!

When the group arrived at the O'Doul house there was not much energy left in the entire troop, so Caroline made a quick trip to the deli to find something suitable for supper. Timothy indicated that he wanted to take Bryan to a real 'fish and chips' pub just down the street for supper, but everyone insisted that this venture could be put off for one day. Caroline returned with a platter of fish specialties (fish taken from the North Sea, Bryan was told), and a heavy vegetable soup that Helen re-heated before the group ate. She insisted that this soup should be eaten only when it was very hot.

The winds outside had picked up and there was on-again, off-again rain. Timothy explained to Bryan that a significant storm had made its way to the Firth of Forth, the bay that connects Edinburgh with the North Sea. It was the 'perfect storm' so far as the local inhabitants were concerned, and it was time to hunker down until this weather passed.

"There is still plenty of time to take Bryan down to the pub," Helen insisted. Timothy agreed, reluctantly. Right after the evening meal, Caroline returned to Manchester.

ↄ҉ҁ   ↄ҉ҁ   ↄ҉ҁ

The next morning the full fury of the storm was exhibited in the neighborhood, including a couple of small downed trees in the street. There were leaves and branches all over the streets and sidewalk and the backyard of the O'Doul house, so this was not a day for sightseeing.

The Guardians were not playing on TV this day, or this evening. "They are going on the road," Timothy informed Helen and Bryan as they were eating breakfast. "I believe that they have to go all the way to Madrid to play a game because the Spanish government is trying to replace bull fighting with professional soccer."

"But they already *have* professional soccer in Spain," Bryan insisted. "I know that for a fact because they regularly beat Team USA in the tournaments."

"What you say may be true," Timothy suggested, "but there is a big push to stop goring bulls in Spain and start kicking soccer shins instead. A large number of the old bull fighting arenas are being torn down in Spain and are being replaced with soccer arenas. It's all part of a scheme to civilize the Spanish population."

"You mean 'civilize' them like what was done in Manchester a couple years ago?" Helen asked. "The game ended in a free-for-all and over a hundred people had to be admitted to the hospital for cuts and bruises."

"But no one got 'gored'," Timothy said. "There is a method to the Manchester madness that we observe on our TV."

"I wonder what they will replace the 'running of the bulls' in Pamplona with, if this changeover occurs?" Bryan asked.

"They will probably have the 'running of the mutton busters' instead," Timothy suggested. "I notice that this is what is happening to American rodeo. We see it all the time on our TV. Everyone says the audience wants less violence. There is a conscious effort to make all the professional sports more civilized, less bloody, and more pleasant."

"Like the 'Last Man Standing Marathon' that comes from Las Vegas," Helen added. "I noticed that the two men who were fighting were inside a cage, and the first person to leave the cage was carried out on a stretcher. Great game!"

"From time to time," Timothy mentioned, "British television shows the story about Bugsy Malone and his attempts to build a gambling paradise in Las Vegas. Near the end of the story the mafia leaders get very angry with him because he has overspent his allocation for the first casino by four million dollars and they pay someone to kill him. The killers go to Hollywood and blow him away. Then, at the end of the picture, the producers mention that the Las Vegas casinos that Bugsy created have grossed more than one hundred billion dollars in profits since he started gambling there sixty years ago. Which goes to show how financially astute the mafia leaders were in those days. Instead of a six million dollar casino he spent ten million, and they killed him. Then they took over his operation and today he has made one hundred billion for them. Some financial geniuses, I would say!"

"New subject," Timothy said. "You mentioned, Bryan, that you all attend a church from time to time in your home in Colorado. What church is that?"

"No, I did not make that statement," Bryan answered. "You were the one who said that you attended the Anglican Church 'some of the time', but I have made no comment about my church attendance. If all the 'goodie' points that I have accumulated toward eternal life are based on my church attendance then I will surely burn in hell."

"You are a 'backslider' then?" Timothy asked.

"Definitely a 'backslider'," Bryan responded.

"But you were one of the faithful at an earlier time?" Timothy asked.

"Definitely," Bryan replied.

"What seems to be your problem?" Timothy asked.

There was a pause in the discussion. "I just don't believe a lot of what I was told the past forty years or so, and I find myself seriously questioning the precepts of the church." starthere

"You are an agnostic?" Timothy asked.

"I am not sure what I am," Bryan responded.

"Do you believe in a God?" Timothy asked.

"I think I believe in a God," Bryan said, "but I wish that he or she had not made such a mess of this planet. The population of this world is out of control, and we don't seem to be able to do anything about it. We talk about the 'dark ages' of fifteen hundred years ago, and yet we live today like we were still in that darkness. We are tolerant of the killing of people on a daily basis so long as that killing does not occur in our little world."

"Is God responsible for all that?" Timothy asked.

"Well he is certainly responsible for *some* of it," Bryan answered.

Timothy sensed that he had hit a sensitive nerve in Bryan's psyche. "Is all of religion phony?" Timothy asked.

There was no reply for a while. Bryan was biting his lower lip as he tried to formulate a coherent statement. "I do not feel that all of religion is phony," Bryan responded, "but I have a hard time separating what seems to be honest religious dissent from the dictates of small organized groups organized to control the actions of larger groups. I am appalled at the efforts of organized religion to apply a series of ecumenical 'dos' and 'donts' or 'litmus' tests to all human beings within their sphere of influence."

"You don't agree with the current Catholic Pope and people like Billy Graham?" Timothy asked.

"That's an easy question to answer," Bryan responded. "The Pope and Billy Graham seem to agree on very little between them. How can I agree with them both when they fail to find common ground for their beliefs?"

"You have a good point there," Timothy said. "But do you advocate doing away with all religion and starting all over?"

Bryan had to laugh. "That is not an option, Timothy, and you know it. Religion has been a dominant force in our lives for thousands of years, and wishing that it would all go away is no answer. It would seem to me that the time we seek true religion is about the time that our children become old enough to begin schooling, and we hope that exposing them to someone's brand of religion will make better people of them. But it doesn't always work that way."

"Adults don't need religion?" Timothy asked.

"Adults may need religion in their lives to carry them through the hard times, but then again, they may not. It's a personal thing. But organized religion does not leave the important questions of life to each person to answer – they form solutions to the questions and offer them to the parishioners as 'gospel' truth. For most people the answers are all 'take it or leave it', and if you leave it you are somehow doomed to an eternity of torment for making the wrong choice."

Bryan continued with, "I also challenge the belief that all goodness and moral stature are taught only in organized religion. No religion can lay claim to the basic laws of mankind found in the Ten Commandments or even the Beatitudes in the Christian New Testament. These rules have been around in many forms for many centuries, and they survive because they are true. Every major religion has their 'rules', and these days the rules are all written down. These rules for living seem to apply whether or not a particular religion is in vogue now or out of vogue. The rules are deemed to be incorruptible, unchanging, everlasting, and explicable."

"You don't like rules?" Timothy asked.

"I don't like rules that can be bent out of shape by Parliaments or Congresses or ecumenical councils. For example, if 'thou shalt not kill' is a basic precept, why do we glorify the killing that occurs in war? Why do we have the audacity to pin medals on people who kill in war time? What is it about our moral weathervane that allows us to point a tank gun at a house in Iraq and blow it to pieces, with bodies flying out of the windows and doors. How can religionists justify that kind of behavior?

"Most religionists do not. How do you justify killing?" Timothy asked.

There was a pause. "In my mind, I separate the dealings that mankind has within his own secular world, using those rules established in tort law, from those dealings that are the outcome of war. War is immoral, no matter how you caste it. And in some cases it is possible to take those who commit war and bring them before a tribunal to judge their deeds according to tort law. But these tribunals have nothing to do with the adjudication of these people as to guilt or innocence in the 'next world'. I don't even believe in a 'next world'. When we die, we die, and our body returns to dust."

"If you bring charges against the 'losers' in a war into the courts, do you also bring charges against the 'winners' in that same war?" Timothy asked.

"To be fair," Bryan responded, "you have to consider both groups for prosecution," Bryan answered. "But we know that the winners will never be prosecuted. I don't have an answer to that question. But my point here is this: no group or no individual has any say about the dispensation of another individual in the 'next world' because there *is* no next world."

"Then Hitler never went to Hell?" Timothy asked.

"Hitler never went to Hell because there was no Hell for him to go to. His body decomposed just like everyone else as soon as the heart pump stopped."

"Doesn't that violate most people's sense of fairness in this world?" Timothy asked.

"I am sure that it does," Bryan answered. "But fairness has nothing to do with it. We are born because of a desire between a human male and a human female to procreate. There is no Godlike decision made here. Either the sperm finds the egg or it does not. If the two find each other than fertilization may occur and the embryo may grow or it may not grow. At the end of a specified period a child may be born, and that child may be 'perfect' in every way or it may have serious defects. God has nothing to do with any of this." endhere

"What about the people who pray?" Timothy asked.

"Are you asking me if prayer changes things?" Bryan asked. "I can answer that question by saying that it all depends on what you are praying for. If you are praying, for example, that you will become a better student to qualify for higher educational training, then the prayer may be just what you need to get up off your rump and make this event happen. It all happens within you and within your brain. You pray to yourself. But you cannot pray for the deliverance of a member of your family or a neighbor from some disease and then expect the disease to leave the member. The life or death of a member is determined solely by the chemical situation that occurs within that member. Don't expect God to answer your prayer."

"Then there is no God?" Timothy asked.

"There may be a God," Bryan answered. "He may have created the heavens and the universe, and he may have allowed mankind to procreate on this planet and gain in wisdom over millions of years. But don't count on God to solve your day-to-day problems and get you or your loved ones out of a health or financial problem. I guess you would say that I believe in an impersonal God."

"Then the New Testament has it all wrong?" Timothy asked.

"Yes, I have to conclude that the New Testament has it all wrong," Bryan responded. "The notion that at one point in time, about 2000 years ago, a man was born in Palestine who had all the answers to the universe and he is able to direct the lives of the five or six billion residents of this earth is foolishness. I don't care what the Pope says, and I don't care what Billy Graham says, it just doesn't add up. If Jesus Christ is the Saviour of this world, where has he been for the past 2000 years? If a quarter of a million people die every day on this earth, how come only a small percentage of them are included in the 'Christian safety net' specified by the New Testament and most of them are left with no champion to support their claims to immortality?"

"You are a terrible cynic, Bryan Wetherington," Timothy said.

"I am a terrible cynic, agreed," Bryan responded.

"Why is religion so popular these days?" Timothy asked.

Again, Bryan had to think a moment. "I think that religion is popular because it fulfills two basic needs of mankind. The first need is 'hope', hope that things will go better tomorrow if they went badly today. The second need is 'escape', and we all use religion to escape from reality."

"What sort of 'escape' are you talking about?" Timothy asked.

"I am talking about the escape mechanisms that we employ whenever we are confronted with a serious problem and we don't know how to solve it," Bryan said. "For example, if we contract a serious disease and no one seems to know how to cure it, we immediately go to a doctor. That doctor may have no clue about how to heal your infirmity, so the two of you drop down on your knees and pray to God that healing will occur. At that point the whole problem has been handed to God and neither you (the patient) nor the curer (the doctor) are responsible for anything that happens in the future. It's now totally up to a superbeing named God to get you out of this mess."

"We use God not only for individual 'escape', but also for entire-nation escape. As soon as we decide to go to war with some other nation we begin praying that God will award us victory and smash our opponents. If there is a God and he is as wise as we would like to think, why would he care who defeated who in the midst of a totally 'economic' war where one side was seeking an advantage over the other side? I read in the newspapers where Mr. Delay, the Republican leader in the House of Representatives, always began every congressional meeting with prayer, asking for guidance from Jesus Christ. Is Jesus Christ *really* available to overcome Mr. Delay's political opponents?"

Bryan wasn't through yet: "When I was a teenager we had a boy in our class named Craig who contracted some kind of rare and terrifying arthritis, and in a period of a couple of years his joints began to seize. By the time we entered the ninth grade he could only move from room to room with crutches and a year later the only way he could write was by putting a pencil between his teeth and bending down and touching the sheet of paper. He and his family were members of our church and the family continued to bring him to Sunday school and the worship service. I remember one Sunday when our Sunday school teacher and the minister stood in front of the church building after the service and spoke at length with Craig about the 'condition of his soul'. They first wanted an assurance that Craig had 'given his life to Jesus Christ in a public profession of faith,' and Craig assured them that he had done this several years earlier. Then they proceeded to explain to him that this catastrophe that had befallen him would not be forever – some day he would be called home to Jesus and he would be 'whole' again."

"A year later his condition became so bad that he was taken to a hospital in Minneapolis-St Paul. I remember that same Sunday school teacher explaining to the rest of us in his class later that 'the Bible says that the sins of the Fathers will be inflicted on the next generation', and this was a good case in point. There was 'sin' in that family and God had demanded retribution. That statement made me so sick that I stood up and headed to the bathroom to vomit. I didn't vomit, but everyone in the class was waiting for me to return. When I returned I looked at the Sunday school teacher and told him, 'That is the biggest piece of happy horseshit that I ever heard in my life, Sir. Craig is dying of arthritis and you want to blame his family for some unnamed sins from the past? Who made you God?'"

"When my parents found out about my outburst they made me go to the Sunday school teacher's home and apologize. I did apologize, but I always felt that I did the right thing the first time."

"You are saying that religion doesn't have answers for life's big problems?" Timothy asked.

"I am saying that formal religion has absolutely *no* answers to life's big questions because the leaders who are trying to formulate these answers are just as fallible as the rest of us. No matter what their original intent may have been, as time goes by they progress up the spiritual ladder and revel in the power that spiritual authority gives them. In the worst case they reach the top rung of their ladder and now they can impose all their thoughts and wishes on the little people below them, claiming that all of this 'understanding' came from God."

"I return to my original question, Bryan," Timothy said. "Is all of formal religion phony?"

"I think not," Bryan responded. "Whatever thoughts you have inside your brain, and whatever decisions you make when you consult with yourself, may represent the closest that you will ever get to communion with the true God who may have created this universe. Everything else is shear folly."

"Have you explained all this to your children?" Helen asked.

Bryan laughed. "No, I have not," he answered. "I know just enough about Christianity to make myself miserable. I know that Jesus may have said that any individual who 'offends' one of these little ones (children), it was far better that an anchor was tied about his neck and he was dropped into the depths of the sea. I can visualize that event, so I am hesitant to instruct my children in my unbelief. After all, I am not infallible either. I may be wrong."

"There are millions of people around us who would tell you that you are wrong," Timothy said. "They make a pretty strong case for the past 2000 years."

Bryan nodded in agreement. "Sometimes organized religion does something good, and I have to give them credit for that," he mentioned. "I remember reading in the National Geographic Magazine about this group of explorers who climbed to the top of some mountain in South America and found the graves of several little children. The children had apparently been sacrificed to some gods by the Indians. When the Catholic Church took charge of religion in South America they banned any more of these human offerings to any gods. So some of the things the Catholic Church has championed seem to be the right thing."

Helen and Timothy agreed. Bryan continued with, "And then, at the same time, some other Roman Catholic group was establishing the legal basis for the Spanish Inquisition and several thousand helpless people were burned at the stake in that country."

"If you were able to, would you ban formal religion in your country?" Timothy asked.

"No, I would not," Bryan replied. "But I would never allow a 'theocracy' to take over my government. I would keep church and state as far apart as possible."

Timothy and Helen seemed to agree with that statement.

"How come you Yanks get into such a frenzy about abortion?" Timothy asked.

"Two reasons," Bryan suggested. "The first one is that we have allowed the natural act of terminating a pregnancy to become a religious issue rather than a health issue, which it really is. The church and those who seek to use the church for their own personal gain have taken charge of the abortion issue and made it what it is today. To some, the 'right to life' argument is the biggest political hatchet in their toolbag. The second reason that abortion remains such a big issue in America is because it is a big money-maker for both the 'right to life' and the 'choice' groups. Americans dump millions of dollars into the coffers of these groups to keep something from happening, and the people who administer these groups know a good thing when they see it."

Bryan continued with, "As the centuries go by, the abortion issue will become less and less contested. As we fill up this planet with human beings, the need to abort unwanted pregnancies will become more obvious. Today the Chinese and Japanese are attempting to control the growth of their populations because of the scarcity of land, and sooner or later America will face the same issue."

"If global warming does in fact become a reality and the level of the oceans rise, then the world population will be left with less and less farmable, livable land, and again, abortion will become a non-issue," Bryan added.

"You Yanks seem to have a terrible time with accepting 'alternative' life styles, like gays and lesbians," Timothy suggested. "Why is there so much smoke and fury in America on these issues?"

"Because, like abortion," Bryan replied, "a segment of the American population has decided to make this a religious issue. And with religious issues you never have to debate in the court of 'common sense'; you can debate solely in an ecclesiastical environment where personal perceptions trump everything else. You can hold a group who has a life style different from your own in total contempt because they don't think like you do. If all else fails you can accuse them of being moral deviants, fornicators, etc. You can imply that they are like the 'Pied Piper of Hamlin', trying to steal children away from their homes and educating them in forms of moral decadence and idolatry. The sad part about this situation is that there are religious leaders who have discovered the 'power' that they can claim if they will organize groups to battle the supposed enemy – the gays and lesbians, etc. These leaders are able to raise vast sums of money to conquer a perceived 'wrong' in American society, and the groups that they lead will call them 'blessed'. Like most issues in this world, they are ultimately economic issues and the people who lead the charges against the alternative life style groups know how to consume the monies they collect.

"Then the gays and lesbians are wrongfully charged?" Timothy asked.

"In the main, yes, this is true," Bryan responded. "Every religious group has to have a 'demon' to overcome, and the gays and lesbians are convenient targets for America's hard conservative 'right'. Gays and lesbians have never been excused from abiding by the laws of the land, so they are not granted special privileges if they declare themselves a part of an alternative life style. Only religious groups choose to defy the law of the land, and they get by with their defiance most of the time. Our principle terrorists in American today are a small band of hard-right extremists who like to hide under the blanket of Christianity. They kill their opposition to save Christianity, just like the Catholic Church did in Spain 500 years ago."

Bryan continued with, "Then there are the outlying members of the Mormon Church who favor polygamy and continue the practice in the rural regions of the Southwest. We don't even know is they are true Mormons or simply religious zealots who can't stand being 'herded' through life by government. The Mormon Church certainly doesn't know what to do with these people. The crazy thing about this issue is that polygamy is really not that big of a deal. If one man can support six wives and thirty kids, what does it matter? Part of the problem with polygamy in the Southwest is that most of the men who continue the practice sign up all their wives and kids for welfare and expect the states to support their families."

"The truth is, if there is a God, he probably doesn't give a damn whether you are a straight, a lesbian, a gay, a pedophile, or what."

It was Helen's turn to speak: "You have come down very hard on Christianity. Have you no good feelings about Jesus Christ?"

Bryan knew that he had to parse his words carefully. He began with, "We teach our children about Santa Claus, the Tooth Fairy, and the Easter Rabbit, even though we know that none of these creatures exist. Then, at about the age of 8 or so, each child figures out that this is all a big spoof and they accept the responsibility of keeping this 'untruth' away from the younger children until they discover the silliness of these stories themselves. But we treat our religion in a completely different way. We meet regularly with other people who have our same 'take' on religion and we expound on the glorious benefits that we have received from being a child of God."

"The problem with this approach is that we never really make contact with God in our entire lives. We pray, but we know that we are praying to ourselves. Prayer is nothing more than an alternative form of 'yoga', where we speak to ourselves. Yoga performs wonders for some people who have problems to resolve because they carefully lay out their options to themselves in their brain and they pick a path to follow. Yoga makes no claims to answering one's difficult personal questions by an intervention from a Godly force."

Bryan continued with, "But Christianity (and all the world's other religions) create a 'listener' who will influence our decisions. The problem is, the 'listener' never responds. When we come to God with a difficult problem to solve, he or she simply tosses the problem back to us and let's us solve the issue ourselves. The great stories in the Old Testament about the men who tested God and got a definitive response are wonderful to read, but they don't make much sense. Did Joshua really march around the city of Jericho seven times and cause the walls to come tumbling down? Did Moses go directly to the next world, avoiding personal death, riding in a chariot of fire? Did Gideon really say to God, 'I am laying a fleece of wool on the threshing floor, and if there is dew on the fleece alone, but nowhere else around the fleece, I will know that you will deliver Israel by my hand?'"

Helen had sat through this entire discussion without saying very much. She showed no surprise at anything that Bryan had said, nor did she seek to correct anything he said. Bryan was not sure if the O'Douls agreed or disagreed with the things he had said, and neither Helen nor Timothy was willing to declare their personal views on these issues up to this point. Bryan felt like he had emptied himself completely of his best and worst emotions, and he got nothing in return.

"You probably don't believe in these people who claim that they can contact the dead, then?" Timothy suggested.

Bryan laughed. "This pseudo-religious activity is about the most blatant and crass display of shyster manipulation of those families left behind by death. However, the people who pay someone to establish this 'contact with the dead' get what they deserve. This mindset also opens the doors to all kinds of multimedia trash that reports the presence of ghosts in a building because the temperature in one of the rooms rises slightly at certain times of day, or the presence of a lightbulb that swings back and forth on certain days of the month. The movies are full of stories about ghosts and demons from hell, all the way from 'The Ghost and Mrs. Muir', which is a pretty harmless story, to vampires and the famous 'Count Dracula'. The 'vampire' cult has encouraged poor people in eastern Europe to hang garlic from the corners of their houses to keep vampires away. What a waste of good garlic!"

"How can you ignore the collected wisdom of 2000 years of scholarly pursuit and the great religious music that has come from the believers, and choose to debunk the Jesus Christ theory?" Helen asked.

For this question, Bryan had an answer. "I am certainly 'uplifted' when I stand and hear the Christmas portion of the 'Messiah' being sung in a cathedral or music hall, but I always wonder why Handel was motivated to create such a masterpiece. True, he was supported by wealthy British who encouraged him to create the oratorios for which he is so famous, but he went far beyond his employer's expectations when he wrote the 'Messiah'. For that matter, Michelangelo went far beyond his employer's expectations when he created the statue of 'David'. He also painted the Sistine Chapel by lying on his back on some rickety scaffolding and personally painted every one of those cute little cherubs on the ceiling."

"But I cringe when I hear about the man who wrote the song, 'Amazing Grace', after he profiteered in the slave trade for so many years. What was his motivation to create this song? Did he do it to pay-back for all his wrongdoings those many years while he sold slaves? Was the purpose of the song to give him a better place in the Kingdom of God, moving him ahead of several thousand people? Was this song going to give him a better 'mansion' in the next world?"

Bryan continued with, "I personally know two elderly people who were so chagrined with their contribution to advancing the cause of Christianity that they sent almost all the money from their retirement funds and social security to a TV evangelist who regularly sent them birthday and Christmas cards to thank them for 'advancing the cause of Christ'. From my standpoint, the TV evangelist was the worst kind of a rip-off artist, and all the elderly people were doing was 'brown-nosing God' to gain a better place in Heaven."

That statement made Helen angry. "You are saying that these elderly people gave money to a religious cause to 'brown-nose' God? That's a terrible thing to say!"

Bryan knew that he had overstepped his bounds. "Okay," he said, "I apologize for making it sound like these elderly people were bad people. But I know for a fact that they talked about having 'many stars in their crowns' and having 'mansions in the sky'. From my perspective, they gave a lot of money to the TV evangelist to 'hedge their bets' on salvation."

There was a pause in the activity. Then Helen asked, "If everything you say is true, what happens at the instant that a person dies?"

"My personal feeling," Bryan responded, "is that as soon as the heart pump stops the brain cannot be adequately cooled, and the body begins to decay quickly. In the matter of a few hours rigor-mortise sets in and the body begins its return to dust."

"But you have said nothing about a 'release' of the spirit at that time," Timothy asked, "in some new dimension that we never see so long as we live, no stopover to separate the good people from the bad people?"

"No, no way-station between the living and the dead," Bryan answered. "There is no 'judgment', no passing into eternal life. Which is probably bad news for a lot of religionists who want special treatment in the 'next world'. I can envision some high-ranking religious leader who has given his entire adult life to the propagation of the Christian, Muslim, or Jewish faith as he understands it, waiting for some 'chariot of fire' to emerge from the clouds to take him home to his reward the instant he dies. Maybe in his earlier dreams he saw a huge congregation of angels who would meet him at the Pearly Gates to welcome him. After all, if he was the leader of a billion converts on earth before he died he deserves some recognition. And he knows that some second-in-command of his organization will stand over his casket for a time, eulogizing about everything that he did during his lifetime. Then a pronouncement will be made that 'he has passed from this earth to his eternal home'. It's the kind of a show that Cecil B. De Mille would have done a great job on. Every movie about ancient Egypt has a scene where the Pharaoh dies and the senior religionist in the crowd announces that 'Pharaoh has gone on to be with his forefathers' while everyone in the scene looks upward."

"Is there no reward for living a good life?" Timothy asked.

"Yes there is," Bryan responded, "and the reward you get is seeing your children and your family living in harmony with those around them when you are alive. If you play the game of life straight, not killing, not stealing, not envying, not taking advantage of those around you, then you have your appropriate reward. Your family members will stand at your graveside and proclaim that you were a good person, and you helped them in their struggles to live a good life."

"You don't like Archbishops and Popes and people like that, do you?" Timothy asked.

Bryan nodded in agreement. "They are the only people I know of who seek to control human thought in the ecclesiastical world. If I were a Shiite Muslim I would probably despise El Sadr and the Imams who control the governments in places like Iraq and Iran."

"Isn't it a little difficult to be so hard on Billy Graham?" Helen asked. "He seems like such a nice man."

"Yes, he is," Bryan replied. "A nice man, but one who is sold on the mystical and the magical. There is nothing mystical or magical about human beings on this earth."

"It is sad to live without 'hope' Bryan," Helen said. "I think I am going to have to keep that 'hope' inside me, someplace. You may be right about all this, or you may be wrong." Bryan agreed.

CHAPTER 7, MATTERS OF WAR

The next morning Bryan looked through the O'Doul house for a computer. He wanted to send a message to Carlie, and email was the easiest way to do that. But he found no computer, so he asked Helen how Timothy had been able to correspond with him in Denver for all these years without a PC. "He goes to work with me," Helen explained, "and uses the computer in the back of the store. The owner has a connection to the internet and we get to use the computer from time to time."

Bryan explained that he would simply write a letter to Carlie and forget about using the internet, but Helen insisted that he and Timothy accompany her to her job and they could use the computer there. "People in the shop stuff information into the computer, but that has nothing to do with the capability of the machine to talk on the internet. Everything happens at the same time. There are other terminals in the store that talk to the central PC all the time."

Timothy liked the idea of going to Helen's work also, despite the fact that the wind was still blowing outside and the road repair and electric people were everywhere in the neighborhood trying to restore all services. Helen called her boss, and he seemed to be agreeable to a visit from Timothy and his American friend, Bryan. Right after breakfast the three left for the tram station.

Bryan noticed that every person in the United Kingdom owns an umbrella. The ladies seemed to prefer small umbrellas, but the men carried large, black umbrellas that caught easily in the wind and whipped about. It was the sort of morning where the umbrella of the person walking next to you was capable of punching out one of your eyes at any moment. Once they arrived at the store, Helen scurried off to begin her day. They were a bit late for work. Timothy took Bryan to the front office and introduced him to Mr. LaPar, the owner. They chit-chatted for a few minutes and then Mr. LaPar took them to the back of the store where an IBM PC was setting on a table. No one was using the PC, but there were several cables attached to the back of the unit. The machine was turned on when the men reached the table. "We keep it turned on all the time," Mr. LaPar told them.

After LePar left, Timothy clicked on the internet button and the internet browser came up grudgingly in about two minutes. The presentation on the screen was a 'Windows' image, but it looked a little different than the image that Bryan was accustomed to in Denver. "I want to show you some of the wonderful things we can do with this machine," Timothy told Bryan. Timothy pecked away at the keyboard and soon the magical name 'Wikipedia' appeared at the top of the screen. Bryan was a little amazed that Timothy knew so much about the PC. "How did you find out about 'Wikipedia'?" Bryan asked.

"Helen showed it to me one day," Timothy responded. "This on-line encyclopedia will tell you anything you want to know about anything. LaPar even lets me use his printer, so once I find something that I like, I can download it immediately. Sometimes, if it is a long report, I print it out and read it at home later."

Bryan had to be impressed. Timothy moved to the 'messaging' section of the computer software, and set up a window where Bryan could write a message to Carlie. Then he jumped up and headed for the kitchenette. "Go ahead and send Carlie a message," he told Bryan. "I am going to the kitchenette for coffee. Do you want coffee?"

Yes, Bryan wanted coffee. "I drink it black," he told Timothy.

"This is English early-in-the-morning coffee, black as the ace of spades, with pieces of grit in the bottom of the cup," Timothy mentioned. "I will bring you a little cream and sugar to take the bite out of the coffee a bit."

Bryan didn't have a lot to report to Carlie. He had arrived safely and he and the O'Douls were having a great time together. He restated the date and time that he would return to Denver, although he had been careful to write that information on the big calendar next to the telephone before he left. He told Carlie that he loved her, and he would be back in Denver soon.

When Timothy returned from the kitchenette he had two cups of coffee with him, a supply of cream, and some sugar cubes. Bryan took one taste of the coffee and put some cream in the cup to soften the affect of the hardrock coffee, but no sugar. Timothy took command of the PC and immediately maneuvered back to Wikipedia. "The first thing I want to show you is some interesting information I found about the Crimean War in the 1850s," Timothy said. "Do you remember that book I sent to you entitled 'The Reason Why – The Story of the Fatal Charge of the Light Brigade' by Cecil Woodham-Smith, an English woman and historian?" Yes, Bryan remembered the book well.

"After I read it I sent it back to you," Bryan mentioned. "And I included a page of questions about what the book said, because the English lingo was a little hard for me to decipher some times."

Timothy did not remember receiving the book back from Bryan. "If the book is lost, I'll replace it," Bryan offered.

No need to do that, Timothy assured Bryan. "I am sure it is somewhere in our library back at the house."

"Cecil Woodham-Smith had a devil of a time getting the information about the Crimean War out of the British War Department so she could prepare the book, and she finally published the text one hundred years after the termination of the war, in the early 1950s. The War Department kept insisting that some elements of the records that Woodham-Smith wanted were still covered by national security concerns, and she had to fight them at least part of the way into the English courts. The courts made fools of the War Department."

"When did Alfred Lord Tennyson write the famous poem about the war, 'The Charge of the Light Brigade'?" Bryan asked.

"Right about the time that the war ended," Timothy answered, "some time around 1854."

"Into the valley of death rode the 600!" Bryan quoted his remembrance of the famous poem.

"The book that Woodham-Smith wrote in the 1950s had a great affect on the manner in which senior officers were chosen for the Royal Army and Navy," Timothy said. "No longer could individuals 'buy' their rank into these military organizations, and the training programs at places like Sandhurst were formalized. To be a general you had to train to be a general. There was no more 'flogging' of enlisted personnel either."

"As I recall," Bryan said, "the leader of the light brigade attacked the wrong target and lost two-thirds of his cavalrymen on a futile charge against Russian artillery."

"You remember correctly," Timothy remarked. "It is a classic study of totally mixed-up communications between a superior commander and his underlings."

Timothy continued with, "The Crimean War is the one where Florence Nightingale emerged as a saviour of injured British troops and the House of Commons got serious about organizing a nursing corps."

There was a pause. Timothy was maneuvering through Wikipedia to find something else.

"What are you looking for?" Bryan asked.

"I am looking for the Boer War," Timothy responded. "There were actually two Boer Wars with a short spell between them when no one was fighting."

"I don't want to be critical of the UK military services," Bryan began, "but it seems to me like the British have a long history of jumping into just about every war that breaks out on this planet. Are you people 'war lovers' or what?"

Timothy turned around from the PC and thought about Bryan's comment for a couple of minutes. "If the truth were known," Timothy said, "us Brits *do* tend to jump into just about every war that comes along, and the reason we do it is because we want to preserve our way of life. We are many people living on some tiny islands next to a war-thirsty continent. We have a little coal deep in the bowels of Wales to heat our homes but no significant manufacturing metals like iron or copper. We can grow food and trees, but that's about all. We end up importing a lot of our food from places like France, which charges us an arm and a leg for that food. We are traders, and we will fight to protect our right to trade with other nations."

"What was the purpose of the Crimean War?" Bryan asked.

"Well," Timothy began, "the Russian Czar was on one side of the fight and the British, French, and the Ottoman Empire were on the other side. It was a fight about who should control the Middle East, and the war ended in a stalemate."

"Why would a fight on the land between Turkey and Russia settle any claims about who was going to control the Middle East?" Bryan asked.

"It was a very complicated situation," Timothy suggested, "and I am not sure whether historians agree about why it all happened."

"This was the war where the officer who led the charge of the light brigade lived on his own private two-masted schooner in the Black Sea. He never had anything to do with the men in his brigade between battles."

"A simplification of the story," Timothy responded, "but there is a lot of truth in that statement."

There was a pause while Timothy displayed the Wikipedia information about the Second Boer War. When it came up on the screen both men read the information carefully. "The First Boer War was very short and both sides shut it down after a year or so. Then there was a ten-year period where England and Belgium discussed their political differences over South Africa while the European farmers there (the Boers) stockpiled weapons and ammunition for another fight. The Boers were armed with Mauser rifles and apparently a few gatling guns that they purchased from the USA. The British Army was extremely successful in scattering the Zulu tribes in South Africa in the years before the Boer Wars because the Zulus only had spears to fight with. The British had rifles. The British totally underestimated the power of the Boers once they were armed with modern weapons."

Timothy continued with, "In 1899 the Boers and the English went at it again, and the English were confident that they would carry the day. They took their regiments into battle with their bagpipers at the lead and on the flanks, and advanced upon the Boers, who held the high ground. Between the Mauser rifles and possibly a gatling gun or two, the British were annihilated, including all the young bagpipers. Public sentiment toward the war shifted in the UK and many citizens insisted that the British Army cease and desist in the effort to overrun the Boers. So the commanding general of the British forces gathered up all the Boer women and children and placed them in a barbed-wire camp 'to keep them safe during the war'. This really raised the ire of the civilian population in the UK. But a year and a half later the Boers ran out of guns and ammunition and the British Army prevailed. As a result, all of Africa between Mount Kilimanjaro on the equator and the northern edge of the Republic of South Africa came under British control."

Timothy continued, "Belgium retained the rights to South Africa, which didn't set well with the financial people in London. They knew that South Africa was destined to become a very wealth country between its gold reserves and its diamonds."

"And Belgium found a way to keep the South African blacks out of the governing process," Bryan added. "They called it 'apartheid'."

Timothy nodded in agreement. "Of course, while we Brits were fighting the Boers, you Yanks were fighting Spain in Cuba to drive the last vestiges of European influence out of the Caribbean. The English newspapers were filled with accounts of 'San Juan Hill' and all that. Wasn't that where Theodore Roosevelt and his 'rough riders' made their mark in history?"

"Indeed, they did," Bryan answered, "and they didn't even have their horses to charge up the hill. The Army made them leave their horses in Tampa, Florida because there were too few ships to transport troops to Cuba."

Bryan continued with, "I think that American historians will always honor Theodore Roosevelt, considering that he began the construction of the Panama Canal, and all that. But 'Teddy' had some personality quirks that defy ordinary reason. For example, he always held that he and his family were protected by some supernatural 'umbrella'. He stated that 'We Roosevelts are always winners in battle!' Well, a few years later his oldest son was killed on a South American 'expedition'. Teddy refused at first to believe that this could happen. His private brand of 'manifest destiny' discounted the death of any of his family in war."

"That doesn't make him a bad person," Bryan added, "but it shows that he wasn't always willing to accept reality."

"I should like to mention that one of the British Generals who fought the Boers in Africa returned to England and founded the 'Boy Scout' effort. His wife supported the 'Girl Scout' effort also. Boy Scouts and Girl Scouts enjoyed a period of great expansion just prior to the First World War."

"What you are telling me is that something 'good' came out of the Boer Wars," Bryan stated.

"Indeed, indeed," Timothy replied.

"I'm not sure if anything good came out of the Spanish-American War," Bryan suggested. "Spain gave the Philippines and Cuba to America, but they also introduced us to yellow fever and malaria, and ninety percent of the fatalities to US soldiers that occurred during that war were from those two diseases."

"But if that hadn't happened," Timothy suggested, "there would never have been a 'Walter Reed Hospital' in suburban Washington, D. C.'"

"Nor a Panama Canal," Bryan added.

There was a pause while Timothy searched for more wars in Wikipedia.

"Did anything good come out of the First World War?" Bryan asked.

"Any historian would have to dig deep to find something good to say about the First World War," Timothy replied. "This was the first war where poisonous gases were used to kill soldiers, and infantrymen were armed with machine guns that fired several hundred rounds of ammunition every minute. Tanks made their first appearance on the battlefield and the artillery found ways to inundate whole square miles of land with enough explosive artillery to kill every living thing in that square."

"The Americans want to take a lot of credit for ending World War One," Bryan said. "Of course, they got into the war quite late."

"Which was the secret of their success," Timothy responded. "If you let several nations fight each other for years and years, both sides lose tons of soldiers and equipment and are soon deprived of any further means of making war. Then, if a new combatant enters the war with fresh soldiers and equipment, they can carry the day."   "Every time I read about World War Two I am surprised at the comparatively short length of time between the end of World War One and the start of World War Two," Bryan said. "It is as if the larger nations of the earth learned absolutely nothing from the First War."

"Perhaps one of the reasons for the quick turnaround in preparation of another war was the fact that Germany quit fighting as soon as the Allies entered its borders," Timothy responded. "Germany suffered much less than France and the Low Countries when the First World War was called to a close."

"I wonder if history would have been written differently if Adolph Hitler had never been born?" Bryan suggested.

"We will never know," was Timothy's reply.

"Winston Churchill was rather famous on both sides of the Atlantic Ocean in those days," Bryan said. "I guess he knew that he had become the Prime Minister of England at just exactly the right time, and British destiny was in his hands."

"Have you ever read any of his works?" Timothy asked.

"Yes, I have," Bryan responded. "It's difficult reading though. I guess he thought on a little higher plane than I."

"I have always thought that 'Winnie' and President Abraham Lincoln had a lot in common," Timothy suggested. "Both of them were looking for Generals who would take command and win a war, and the Generals continued to 'crap in their hats' regularly. For example, most British civilians still do not understand why the debacle at Dunkirk occurred early in the Second War.

"What do Americans think about President Harry Truman?" Timothy asked.

"He made some brave decisions in this time as President," Bryan replied, "but as time went by he lost his fire and fury and acquiesced on several issues."

"Like?" Timothy asked.

"Like when he decided to drop the Hiroshima and Nagasaki atomic bombs," Bryan answered. "That took a lot of courage. He also showed great political courage when he traveled to South Korea and fired General MacArthur on the spot. MacArthur was a real asshole, and everyone knew it."

Bryan continued with, "After the MacArthur incident, the President became so involved with infighting in Washington that he was probably glad when his turn as President was up and he could go home to Missouri."

"There are some parallels between the First World War and the Gulf War in which we participated," Timothy said. "In both cases the political powers who were left standing deemed that there had been enough bloodshed and they shut down the war before it moved into its next phase. In World War One there was no move on the Allies part to enter Germany and destroy its industrial capacity. In the Gulf War you and I were stopped south of Baghdad and told to go home because Saddam Hussein had now learned his lesson and he would return Iraq to a peaceful nation. We knew that the decision was foolishness, but we could do nothing about it. We work for a President; he doesn't work for us. Beside, at that point both of us were alive and well, and any further 'warring' could do us in. If I had left Iraq a month earlier I would probably have my legs today."

"Have the UK, the USA, and Western Europe learned their lesson about war?" Bryan asked. "We call ourselves the 'center of Christianity' in the world and yet we constantly seek new and devious ways to make war around the planet. If the Christians of this earth make war all the time, is it any wonder that the Muslims are following our lead?"

"It's time to break out in a rendition of 'Where Have All the Flowers Gone?'" Timothy suggested. "Long time passes."

"God bless the Kingston Trio."

Timothy raised his right hand and index finger. He had thought of something significant to say. "You asked if anything good came out of the First World War – well, I just thought of something. Before World War One every wealthy family in the UK had tons of servants to take care of their homes, their farms, and their businesses. Labor was cheap. In 1914 a call went out to young people to either join the military forces or start producing war material, and hundreds of thousands of people who were deemed unfit for active duty soon began manufacturing weapons, ammunition, packaging food, sewing uniforms, and performing every other task necessary to support a marching army. As a result, the wealthy people of the UK were soon left with a handful of old servants who stuck around solely because they had been promised some kind of a retirement some day. All the middle-aged and young people left. As a result, after the war, the number of servants who served the very rich decreased significantly. For example, most of the 'nannies' disappeared from the labor scene. They made five times as much money stuffing gunpowder into an artillery round."

"New subject," Bryan said. "When did the British figure out that their days were numbered in India?"

Timothy thought for a few moments. "Who ever named 'India' the 'Jewel in the Crown' named it well," he said. "India was an unending source of raw materials for the British industries throughout England, Scotland, Ireland, and Wales. The British did whatever they had to do to keep the shipping lines between India and the UK open at all times. For example, though they did not participate in the building of the Suez Canal, they bought-up all the outstanding shares of private stock in the canal as soon as it was built and took control of the canal away from the French. No wonder the French hate our guts," Timothy suggested.

"We built a pretty good railway system in India, but every one of those tracks served one common purpose – to get those raw materials from the source to the docks. We allowed the Maharajahs to continue to operate the local governments for their own good and we established enclaves in the more desirable parts of the country to preserve a bit of the British way of life in a wretchedly poor country."

"Then along came Mr. Gandhi," Bryan said.

"Yes, along came Mr. Gandhi," Timothy repeated. "But by the time he arose to significant political power in India the British 'grasp' on meaningful political control was waning. I think the Londoners knew that all was not well in eastern India in the heat of World War Two when the Japanese were able to overpower large Indian fighting forces that should have been able to stop the Japanese in their tracks. The truth was, the Indian military forces trained by the Crown didn't give a damn at this point. To them, one conqueror was just as good as another. What the British citizenry in the UK did not hear about was the common practice of 'fragging' British officers in the midst of battle. They were shot in the back or killed with grenades by their own Indian soldiers."

"When India declared its independence in 1947 there were very few British who thought that the Crown had gotten a bad deal from India. It was time for us to leave."

"New subject," Bryan said. "Should we be afraid of the Muslims?"

"Oh yes, very much so," Timothy replied. "There is no way we can 'out-Jesus' them because they promise the same 'eternal life' that Christianity offers. We cannot 'out-pray' them because they pray five times a day. We may not be able to outspend them because they control most of the world's oil. We can't defeat them in war because many of them are anxious to die in battle."

"But there is one thing we can do to defeat them," Timothy surmised. "It's the same thing we're trying to do with the Chinese right now. We must flood them with this world's goods and make them as materialistic as we are. The Muslim religion can withstand most anything, except unending prosperity, just like the Chinese."

The PC session was over. Timothy, Helen, and Bryan ate lunch at a tea room across the street from the dry cleaners, and then Timothy and Bryan prepared to return to the O'Doul house. "We will pick up food for tonight," Timothy suggested.

"No," Helen suggested, "tonight is another 'pub' night. The Guardians are playing on the big TV at the 'War Horse', and the three of us need to go there. I'll be home at 6 and the game starts at 7."

On the way back to the house, Timothy suggested that they stop at a gift shop across the street from the tram station. "Do you want to take home any souvenirs of the UK?" Timothy asked Bryan.

"Not particularly," was Bryan's reply. Then he remembered that he should buy something nice for Helen since the O'Douls were caring for him this entire week. There was an advertisement on the tram that caught his eye also – a small electric car where two people sat side-by-side (there was no back seat), and the accelerator pedal and brakes were all mounted around the steering wheel. It was about the size of a golf cart but it had sheet metal, plastic, and windows all around to keep the weather out. He had carefully copied down the telephone number and intended to call the agent as soon as they reached the house. Since the O'Douls never roamed past the city limits of Edinburgh in a car, he knew that the little electric car might be the perfect transportation vehicle for them.

Bryan made a mental note of the nicer gifts that they found in the gift shop, and then the two of them walked to the house. Timothy was in great spirits. "Helen will be taking me to the Army Clinic tomorrow morning," Timothy told Bryan. "I have to schedule medical appointments far in advance, so I couldn't change this one at the last minute. We'll only be gone for three or four hours," he said.

Bryan saw this as an opportunity to check into the electric car business. As soon as they reached the house, Bryan waited until Timothy stepped into the bathroom and then he quickly dialed the number of the electric car agent. A young lady answered, and then referred him to a salesman named Roger Pilkington.

"Roger," Bryan began, "how can I get a good look at the little electric car that you advertise on the tram – the two-door?"

"We're right downtown," Roger answered, "just across the street from the County Administration Building."

"I am a stranger in town," Bryan said, "and I must return to the States in two days. The people that I am staying with need a car, and they are older. How far can you travel in that electric car?"

"About 60 miles," was the answer, "in stop-and-go traffic. In the countryside you might make 90 miles."

"Do I dare ask what the price is?" Bryan asked.

There was a pause. "The basic car sells for 3000 pounds sterling, which is about 6000 dollars American. But you probably want the model that has air conditioning on it, and it costs another 500 pounds."

Yes, Bryan was definitely interested. "Does it plug directly into house AC power?" Bryan asked.

"Absolutely, Sir," was the answer. "You just plug it in every night, and by the next morning the battery is back to full power."

"Would it be possible for you to bring one of those cars tomorrow morning to where I am staying?" Bryan asked. "This is a surprise, and I want to make sure that the people I am staying with have left the house before you come."

"What's the address?" Roger asked. Bryan gave him the address of the O'Douls. "How would you be paying for this car?" Roger asked.

"With the only money that I have on me," Bryan answered, "and it's called a VISA card." There was a stir at the other end of the line and Roger asked if it would be all right if he called Bryan back in a few minutes. "Do you want me to bring a particular color car?" Roger asked.

"Any color will do, but bring a brochure that shows all the colors that the car comes in. Then the O'Douls can pick out the color they like later. Please come around 10 a.m. and bring all the paperwork that I must sign to buy the car."

"What is your full name, Sir?" Roger asked.

"Bryan Allen Wetherington, Denver, Colorado," was the reply. "When you call back, just ask for me, Bryan Wetherington. Just say 'yes', which means that you will be here at 10 o'clock tomorrow, or 'no', which means that you can't make it."

Then Bryan remembered that he wanted to ask about the possibility of placing special controls on the car such that the driver could drive and stop without the use of his legs. "Yes Sir," Pilkington replied, "this car was originally designed in Switzerland for handicapped people, and there is an adapter kit called a 'motorcycle option' that can be installed on the car. I only have one of these cars in stock, but I can bring that one to show you if my management is agreeable."

"I will call back in about fifteen minutes," Roger said. Then the telephone went dead.

When Timothy came into the living room he saw Bryan putting the receiver back on the hook. "Did someone call?" he asked.

"I just made a phone call down the street," Bryan answered. "The man will call me back in a few minutes."

"Do you want something to eat before we go to the War Horse Pub?" Timothy asked. "Perhaps 6:30 is a bit late for your supper. I can find something to tide you over until we go down to the pub. We still have some cherry pie left over from last Thursday."

No, there was no need to eat now. It was early afternoon.

Bryan spent the rest of the afternoon looking at the O'Doul collection of books in their library. The older books were all bound, some of them in elegant materials like leather. There was a second printing of 'Pride and Prejudice' on the shelf – obviously an important item in the O'Doul collection. But the newer books were paperbacks, like the 'Penguin' books, and all the Agatha Christie mystery stories. There were also some modern books, like P. D. James' 'Adam Dowgleisch' mystery series and Dan Brown's 'The DaVinci Code'. Harry Potter had not yet made it into the O'Doul collection.

"Did you find a book to read tomorrow?" Timothy asked Bryan. No, Bryan had not. "We can go to the pub early," Timothy suggested, "and spend a few minutes at a bookstore close to the pub. They have all the popular fiction there, including the London best sellers. You may even find some of the 'New York Times Best Sellers' there also."

"I may re-read 'Pride and Prejudice'," Bryan said.

"Excellent choice," Timothy answered. "The copy that we have is quite old and worn, but the text is easy to read because they printed it in large fonts in those days."

            ℰℛ   ℰℛ   ℰℛ

As soon as Helen came home from work she began scurrying about to get everything done before they left for the War Horse Pub. Her biggest concern was collecting up a series of pillboxes that they would have to take with to the doctor the next day. Since Timothy had said that he took very few pills, Bryan wondered what this was all about.

They left the house at 6:30 and made their way to the pub. Apparently Helen had called the owner because one corner of the War Horse Pub was already marked with a 'reserved' sign. "There have been some changes since the last time we were here," Helen mentioned. "They used to have only one big TV screen, but I see that they now have screens on all four walls, high up where everyone can see them. Before, when it got crowded, it was hard to see the one screen mounted near the door."

Timothy ordered fish and chips for the trio and brown beer. The owner mentioned that the pub also had 'light' beer if anyone wanted it, and they also had some cold beer in bottles. Bryan was tempted to try some of the cold beer, but he noticed that Timothy was determined that he (Bryan) should sample the true warm, brown brew for which every pub in the UK is famous. So he settled in with warm beer.

As soon as the beer was served, Timothy raised his glass, looked at Helen and Bryan, and proclaimed, "We dedicate this pint in honor of Brigadier Galliard-Trimble, the last man to die in the Gulf War! May his soul rest in peace."

Hear, hear!

One more time the Guardians won on the TV, and they did so without any side-battles in the stands. It should not have surprised Bryan that the game proceeded without incident because Manchester won by four goals and every tenth person in the stands seemed to be a constable.

They returned to the house around 10 p.m. and sat down in the living room to review the day's activities. But Timothy was well on his way to sleep so the party broke up. "We will see you in the morning," Helen said, "about 8 a.m. We will leave for the doctor's office at 9 a.m."

As she was leaving the room, she turned and mentioned, "A Mr. Pilkington called just as we were leaving the house, and he says 'yes' he will do what he said he would do. Apparently he had a problem getting through on the telephone earlier in the evening. "Thank you," Bryan replied. Then they all went to sleep.

CHAPTER 8, TRUTH TIME

The next morning breakfast proceeded on schedule, the dishes were loaded into the dishwasher, and the O'Douls were on their way to the doctor sharply at 9 a.m. Bryan wondered if he had made a bad choice in planning to read 'Pride and Prejudice' because the font in which the book was printed was totally obscure from Bryan's viewpoint. This book was a hundred years old, at least. The publishers in that day and time used sweeping, oversize letters to begin each paragraph, much like one would see if you tried to read a page from the Guttenberg Bible.

Mr. Pilkington was right on time, however. At ten a.m. Bryan noticed a bright yellow car pulling up to the house, and a tall young man emerged from the vehicle in a suit. Bryan immediately put away his book and started toward the front door. When the doorbell rang he was already putting on his coat. Pilkington introduced himself and the two men returned to the canary yellow car at the curb. Pilkington opened the door on the driver's side and invited Bryan to drive. Once Bryan was seated and had moved the seat forward to reach the brake pedal, he noticed the special controls around the steering wheel. "The grip on the left is the brake," Pilkington said. "This car has power brakes even though it is extremely light in weight. The driver can stop the car easily with his left hand."

"The speed setter for the right hand rotates just it does on a motorcycle, and as soon as the driver touches the brakes the speed setter returns to the 'idle' setting. This is a well designed machine," Pilkington said.

"How much extra does the 'motorcycle option' cost?" Bryan asked.

"Three hundred pounds was the answer.

"Does this car have air conditioning?" Bryan asked.

"Yes Sir, it does."

"Then let's drive it," Bryan suggested. He didn't want to drive very far because he wasn't accustomed to driving on the left side of the street, but he wanted to convince himself that this car was a real car, not a toy. Halfway to the tram station he did a 'U' turn and proceeded back to the house.

Pilkington was pleased. "Sold, Mr. Pilkington," Bryan told him. "Let's go inside and do all the paperwork."

While Roger Pilkington was at the house, he made an inspection trip to the garage. He determined that a new electrical line should be run from the main power box at the back of the house to the garage so the car could be charged up every night. "Since Mr. O'Doul is handicapped," Pilkington said, "the power company picks up the tab for the new electric outlet."

Bryan was trying to figure out a smooth way to transfer this car to the O'Douls, and the only thing he could think of was this: Get the O'Douls into a hack to take the three of them to the Edinburgh train station the morning that Bryan had to leave for London. He had to allow at least an extra hour to give Pilkington time to show them what cars were available at the dealership, and then he would ask Pilkington to return them to their house later in the day. Pilkington expected the delivery time of the car to be about six weeks, and during that time the O'Douls could sell their old car.

Pilkington took Bryan's VISA card and gingerly transferred all the data to a form that he had brought from the dealership. "How can I tell my wife back in Denver that I have bought a car with our VISA here in Edinburgh, and the cost is going to be close to eight thousand dollars?" Bryan asked Roger.

Roger had an immediate answer: "As soon as I return to the dealership I will send an email to your wife and inform her of the sale so she won't be shocked when she sees the charge on your VISA card." That seemed like an excellent plan to Bryan.

"Would you write down exactly what you want me to say in the email?" Roger asked. "I also need your email address."

Bryan wrote a fairly long letter to Carlie, explaining that he wanted to present the O'Douls with a tiny, new electric car that would enable them to get around Edinburgh. He would pay the VISA bill when it arrived with that pesky General Electric stock that he had held for so many years – the stock was worth well over $12,000.00 now. He ended the letter with the words, 'I wanted to do something nice for this man and his wife. He has been my friend for a long time.'"

When all the paperwork was signed, Roger Pilkington prepared to leave. "The exact cost of the taxes for this car will be determined later, but I think I can guarantee you that the sale of the old car will more than cover the taxes on the new car. The government will pay the O'Douls a stipend directly for buying an electric car since the UK is anxious to get people out of their old, smog-causing motor vehicles."

A copy of all the paperwork and the brochure showing all the available colors of the car was placed into a file folder by Pilkington and handed to Bryan. "We will see you at the dealership tomorrow," Pilkington said. Then he turned and left.

Everything was in place.

℘   ℘   ℘

When Helen and Timothy returned from the doctor they were not in very good spirits. They had returned much later in the day than they had expected. While they were changing clothes, Bryan walked down to the tram station and delicatessen and bought food for the evening meal. Helen seemed to be especially depressed by the day's events, and Bryan didn't want to ask her to cook.

They ate the evening meal quietly. Then they retired to the living room and Helen brought tea for everyone. "Timothy has some things to tell you, Bryan," Helen said. "We learned a lot at the doctor's office today."

Bryan waited. "The doctor told me today that his original prognosis is now confirmed," Timothy began, "and my left lower leg is now inflicted with cancer in the bone. He cited several possible ways to attack the cancer, but he recommends chemotherapy and radiation immediately. He wanted me to start the treatments right now, but I told him that you were here and I want to wait until next week. That didn't seem to bother him a great deal."

"You had some idea that this might be the case when you invited me into your home last month?" Bryan asked.

"Yes, we did," Helen answered. Bryan remembered that Carlie also had a feeling that there was more to the invitation for Bryan to come to the UK than what met the eye. "I'm sorry to hear that you are so sick," Bryan began, "but I'm glad that you asked me to come here at a time when you seem to be feeling well. We have spent a lot of time together, but this past week has to be the best. Thank you for the invitation; I'm glad that I came."

"I'm going to have to renew my membership at the Anglican Church," Timothy mentioned. "It wouldn't be fitting to walk away from the church at a time like this."

Timothy paused, and then continued. "If you hadn't come now I would have had to look for you in the next world. How could any gatekeeper at the Pearly Gates refuse admission to a couple of old gunnery sergeants who did everything that their country and their church asked them to do on the field of battle? They told us to go forth and kill and maim and we went there and we killed and we maimed. Would some archbishop or pope or evangelical minister wave incense over our graves to smooth our way into the next world? Have we no claim to a life after death?"

Another pause. Then Timothy began with "No, I don't really think that any of us has any claim to a home beyond the skies. We are no different in that respect than the smallest field mouse who dies in the backyard and his body slowly decomposes to salts and ashes. What right do we have to claim everlasting life when every other species on the face of the earth is denied that same honor? Should I shake my fist at this elusive God that I claim to worship, and shout up at him that he never gave me a *chance* to succeed in this life? After all, God, you took my legs away and I have no means of transport left except by making my way precariously down the sidewalk on a couple of steel appendages."

"But I don't think that God short-sheeted me," he continued. Hell, I have had a lifetime of joy watching the kids grow up and blossom into responsible human beings. And I have spent years and years with this woman who sleeps beside me every night, when I had two legs and when I had no legs. I could never have made it this far without her."

Suddenly, there was a dramatic change of pace. Timothy was smiling again. "What's on our agenda for tomorrow?" he asked.

CHAPTER 9, REVELATIONS

There was no use to talk about medical problems any more. Timothy had played his trump card when he told Bryan that he would soon be in treatment for bone cancer, and Bryan assumed that this type of cancer was about as serious as a disease became, something akin to cervical cancer among women. One question that Bryan did not ask and Timothy did not offer to discuss was how long it took for bone cancer to claim its victim. From the look on Helen and Timothy's faces when they returned from the doctor, it was obvious that a quick and easy recovery was not one of the options.

The evening was getting late, but there were more items to discuss. Bryan opened the next discussion with, "Tomorrow morning we go to the train station and I begin my trip back to the States. We should take a hack to the station because my suitcase is large, and I want to stop off at an agency close to the train station and show you something."

"Something like what?" Timothy asked.

"It's a secret," Bryan responded. "I just want to show you something that I found advertised on the tram. We can go by the store and see the item, and then I have to catch the 11 a.m. train to Heathrow."

This secrecy had piqued the O'Douls' interest.

While they were all sipping their tea, Timothy began to discuss what the future held for himself and Helen. He totally ignored his cancer situation – all his thoughts were about their plans for a family reunion in one of the beach cities near Southampton several months from now. Obviously they had visited this resort before because Timothy knew exactly what they would do after they got there. Helen had some nice things to say about the villa where they always stayed, how it was so well maintained and the flowers were always so beautiful.

"What are your vacation plans?" Timothy asked Bryan.

"We don't have a regular place where we go to vacation," Bryan answered. "For a long time we kept a timeshare in Breckenridge, Colorado but we sold that two years ago. Neither one of us cares to ski that much any more. For one thing, the annual fees to maintain a timeshare at a popular ski resort have gotten a little out of hand."

"Are you confident about the economic future of your state and the nation at this time?" Timothy asked.

"Not particularly," was the reply. "Most Americans have acquired far too many of this world's goods on credit, and there is going to be hell to pay someday for our indulgences."

"We Brits indulge a lot too," Timothy suggested.

"So I have noticed," Bryan responded. "The Wall Street Journal says that America and the UK are in a neck-and-neck race to see who can outspend the other for stuff that we don't need."

"I wonder if China will put us both under?" Helen suggested. "Since one-fourth of the people in the world are Chinese, they are going to have a lot to say about how this world operates in the future."

Everyone agreed with that statement.

"For right now, the Chinese are depending on both the USA and the UK to provide them with management expertise to get their national industries moving," Bryan stated. "But that won't last forever. Right after World War Two we Americans laughed at the attempts of the Japanese to 'mimic' what we did in America, and then fifty years later they create and fabricate electronic devices like America can not imagine. The Chinese are just as smart as the Japanese, and right now they have vast amounts of American dollars to spend on their industries."

"The only thing that will slow down the Chinese progress toward modern industrialization is their insatiable lust for more land and more control over the nations who surround them," Bryan suggested. "India and Pakistan will always keep their nuclear weapons 'at the ready' so long as China keeps trying to expand their common borders. The worst thing that could happen in the lower Asian subcontinent is that India and Pakistan turn on one-another."

China would love that," Timothy suggested.

"Meanwhile," Helen asked, "what is going to happen in America?"

Bryan rumpled up his nose while he debated what answer to give. "Americans continue to live out the fantasy that they are smarter, tougher, and more forward-looking than any other nation on the earth. Americans concede a certain amount of 'smarts' to countries like the UK, central Europe, Japan, China, and Korea, but they refuse to believe that countries like India could ever surpass the USA in industrial and business growth. Right now we are seeing that this is not true any longer. India is the biggest democracy in the world and they are beginning to exercise their strengths, just as China has done."

Bryan continued with, "We Americans have always looked to places like the UK and Canada to see how their social 'experiments' and attempts at increasing trade with other nations go. In the next few years we will have to completely rework our medical systems in the States, and the medical practices in place in Canada, UK, France, Germany, and the Scandinavian countries are our best models. But American pride, especially as seen in the Congress of the United States, is so great that there are Americans who would try to invent a whole new medical system to replace the conglomeration that we now have, just to spite the rest of the world. In this case, attempts at 'Yankee ingenuity' will cost America a fortune."

"Then medicine in America will be 'socialized'?" Helen asked.

"Eventually," Bryan replied. "It bothers me greatly to hear politicians at the national and state levels heap scorn on the medical efforts of the other G-8 countries, implying that the systems they have introduced are 'inferior' and provide substandard medical and dental services to their people. I have spent my entire adult life participating in a 'socialized' medical system called the U. S. Military and occasionally the Veterans' Administration, and I love it. When Carlie and I get old enough we'll go into Medicare, and I see no reason why I shouldn't love that too."

"There are two classes of politicians who cause more harm than good in the national discussion over medical services," Bryan said. "The first group heaps ridicule on the federal agencies that service Medicare and Medicaid, implying that these groups are nothing more than a bureaucratic morass that spends more money than it should to service the American people. They imply that these government groups are inept and unable to cope with modern medical needs. The second class of useless politicians are the ones who imply that a single-payer medical system will cost much more than what Americans are spending today, that only a private payer such as Aetna or Cigna or the other big hospital corporations know how to control medical spending."

"We saw what happened when the federal government tried to shift seniors from Medicare to private medical plans a few years ago. The private plans kept all the 'well' people who cost them very little, and sent back the 'sick' people to Medicare for treatment. Then some Congressmen wanted to 'crow' about the fact that private medical firms performed their medical tasks using less money than the government! What a farce!"

"Is health care going to cost Americans more than what you spend today?" Helen asked.

"Absolutely," Bryan responded. "No medical services are free. Americans will have to pay more in federal taxes to support an all-inclusive medical system in America because so many more people in America will have medical coverage, and any thinking person knows that."

"You said something a couple of days ago about the abortion issue in America," Timothy said. "Will abortion services be included under the 'medical' umbrella?"

"I don't think so," Bryan answered. "As I said yesterday, neither side, the 'right to life' or the 'right to choice' group will stop doing what they are doing because it generates such large revenues for themselves. But the 'morning after' pill is changing the way young women live their sexual lives, and I would assume that America will follow the footsteps of France in this matter – putting the decision of abortion back into the 'rights' column of the individual woman. Beside, when America begins to fill up with people like the large cities in India have, and there are homeless people living and dying on the streets every day, the decision of whether or not a woman should terminate her pregnancy will be delegated to the woman personally, not to religious groups or some state legislatures. If this does not happen then our cities will become 'baby mills' just like the poor neighborhoods in Mexico City next to the city dump where children forage for food and mom delivers a new baby every year."

"What about the loss of manufacturing jobs and the decrease in the lower-middle economic groups in the US and the UK?" Helen asked.

"Those trends are going to continue," Bryan said. "Rich Americans will continue to ship manufacturing jobs to third world countries because the final products are produced more cheaply. What those rich Americans are ignoring is the fact that Americans will eventually reach the point where they can no longer afford to buy all the gadgets manufactured in the third world because they have no jobs here in America. At that point, 'consumerism' has to take a kick in the pants, and fewer and fewer Americans will be able to buy all the latest and greatest gadgets because they have no money. Being poor is a real 'downer'."

Bryan wasn't finished. "There are some naïve Americans who think that we as a nation can continue to create new and exciting products that the rest of the world will buy from us. What they are overlooking is the fact that the industrialists in this country always go to a third-world location to manufacture their gadgets and even the design of these products is being moved off shore. We Americans think we are the only ones who know how to design great products – well, we delude ourselves. Have you noticed that General Motors is moving all its 'sedan' design to eastern Europe and only its truck design will remain in America? In twenty-five years the only thing that American labor will contribute to the vehicle world is the assembly of those vehicles in places in America where the cost of living is the least. For a time South Carolina, Alabama, Mississippi, Kentucky, and Texas folks will catch a windfall of revenues from assembling vehicles and the vehicle-building states that we know today, like Ohio and Michigan, will dry up and become pastureland, just like they were two hundred years ago."

"It's going to be that bad?" Timothy asked.

"That bad," Bryan responded. "The only thing that will keep the rust belt alive is iron and steel production."

"Would an infusion of money into the education arena stave-off some of this?" Helen asked. "We in the UK are planning huge upgrades in our educational systems to provide a better working force for business and industry."

"It certainly might help," Bryan responded. "But in America, what we are seeing is a yawning group of high school and college students who are just marking time in their classes, awaiting the day that someone will hand them a diploma so they can go out in the world and make big money. We have a class of kids now who think that the most important skill they can learn right now is how to play the TV games on their X-Boxes or Nintendos. The Army is distributing TV war games so the teenagers will see how great it is to do battle, hoping that they will volunteer for military service when they graduate from high school."

"There are some cynics who have envisioned a world fifty years from now that basically includes five groups," Bryan said. "The first group is the financial group who will live around Manhattan Island and buy and sell all sorts of fiduciary documents that they hope Americans will buy, like stocks, bonds, etc. They will provide all the banking services. The second group is the service group who will deliver pizzas in the early evening, clean your house, wash your car, drive trucks, and handle retail sales. The third group includes the medical folks who will work to keep you alive as long as possible. The fourth group is the educational group who will compete for students at the high school and college levels. The fifth group is the military group who will protect our country. That's the sum total of the people who will work in America in fifty years."

"I find that hard to accept," Timothy responded. "You said nothing about engineers, designers, and technicians."

"Today," Bryan answered, "a bright young engineer in India fights to get to the USA to work. Could it be, fifty years from now, that the bright young American engineers will be fighting to get to China to work in the design and manufacturing world?"

"This entire notion seems a little ridiculous," Timothy suggested. "I notice that you did not mention the 'clergy'."

"The clergy will still be here," Bryan replied. "I should have included them as a sixth group. As times get tougher and tougher more Americans will look for more avenues of 'escape', and religion offers more escape than any other group in the world. Religion is also the greatest source for 'hope' in the future. But 'hope' doesn't solve ones pressing problems. When Americans cannot solve their greatest problems they will turn to an all-powerful God whose job is to save them from ruin. There will be preachers on every street corner and on every TV set, advising the public that they can still save themselves if they return to God in penance. Many will believe, but the hard times will continue. Recall in the Old Testament that some of the Children of Israel spent 300 years in bondage, awaiting the Messiah. Our 300 years has not yet begun."

"Do you foresee a time when the USA could be overrun by another nation?" Timothy asked.

"There is no reason for it *not* to happen in the distant future," Bryan responded. "Remember that America owns a large portion of the farmable land in this world, and there are nations who would kill to take that land. Such invaders would be pleased to destroy our manufacturing capability and our citizens, but the land is far too valuable to destroy."

"So what nation is going to be the world's 'top-dog' a hundred years from now?" Timothy asked.

"Tough call," Bryan responded. "I really don't see any one nation standing out, head and shoulders above all its competitors. For one thing, all those nations will have access to the same kinds of information, and information breeds wisdom and wisdom breeds strength. In terms of calling all the shots in the world, a conglomeration of nations will probably do the job. I think America and the UK will both be players in the 'world conglomeration', but neither will be predominant in the scale of things."

"Will any Muslim nations, like Saudi Arabia move to the top of the heap?" Timothy asked.

"No," Bryan answered emphatically. "Any nation that excludes half of its adult population from any interaction with business, industry, and government will lag far behind the nations who try to include everyone in their decisions. In a sense the Muslim world is a copy of the American Indian world that the Europeans found when they began to conquer America and make it a white person's domain. American Indian men despised their women and tried to live off the 'fat' of the land. It didn't work. They died off from disease and infighting while the white man grew ever stronger in America. The American Indians have no claim to greatness today and neither do any of the Muslim countries."

"Even the Muslim countries who own most of the oil?" Helen asked.

"Even those countries," Bryan responded. "None of us will be here one hundred years from now, but there is every reason to believe that most of the Muslim nations will be nothing but dried up oases on a continent of sand. Only those Muslim nations who invest in the world around them will save themselves, like Qatar."

"Who will be the richest family in America fifty years from now?" Timothy asked.

Bryan smiled. "Whoever this richest family is, they will have to be tied closely to the oil, natural gas, and future energy developments around the world. The Bush family has closely allied themselves with Saudi Arabia for that reason, and they will continue to flourish in America so long as the oil holds out. But there are other American families that have learned how to 'make a buck' in a hurry, so the Bush family will have a lot of competition.

"The richest family in the world fifty years from now may reside in India or China, since collecting outlandish wealth depends on the availability of cheap labor. Only China and India have the volume of cheap labor that world-class entrepreneurs seek."

"Will China's addiction to communism hold them back in the world's race for the title of the 'most affluent and most prestigious nation on the earth'?" Timothy asked.

"I think not," Bryan responded. "The Chinese have tried several forms of government over the past 5000 years, and nothing they have tried to date has satisfied their people for any great length of time. True communism (if there is such a thing as 'true communism') will yield to a more liberal form of government in China as time goes by. The 'whiff' of capitalism that the Chinese people have experienced in the last twenty years will make them more and more anxious to trash the communist view of life. After all, communism depends on all of its converts to be poor, and there is a rising middle class in China that won't stand for communism forever. The Chinese also have an outstanding work ethic that serves them well."

"What about the American work ethic?" Timothy asked.

"Americans continue to have the potential to do great things in this world," Bryan responded, "because they are 'unshackled' and some Americans have learned to look into the future to guess how their businesses should operate. We honor this country's thinkers, young or old, who are willing to take a chance and offer the public something new. But the thinkers are few and the sitters in America are legion. America is creating a lot of people right now who will be poor forever, and most of them don't have an inkling of how to get out of that circle of poverty. Truly, America's middle class is an endangered species today."

"Are you related to Nostradamus in any way?" Timothy asked.

Bryan laughed loudly. "Not that I know of," he answered.

"Will modern medicine have a cure for the common cold a hundred years from now?" Timothy asked.

Again, Bryan laughed loudly. "I doubt it," was his reply.

⁊ ⁊ ⁊

The next day, everything went smoothly. Helen called a hack and the trio made their way downtown. Bryan led them into the dealership and Mr. Pilkington showed the O'Douls the line of electric cars that he had in the showroom. The O'Douls were excited by all the attention that the salesman was giving them, but they were also confused. Helen caught on pretty quickly, but Timothy remained confused.

"Is this salesman trying to sell us a car?" Timothy asked Bryan.

"No, the car has already been sold," Bryan explained. "Your job is to pick out the color you like, and the salesman will arrange to drive you home in it."

"You bought us a car?" Timothy exclaimed. "Why did you do this?"

"Because I want to cement our friendship with a gift, and the gift that seems to be the most appropriate at this time is a new car."

Pilkington explained to the O'Douls that an electrician would come to their home and install a new electrical line in the garage to charge up their car every night. He also explained that the federal government was offering stipends to people who would buy and drive electric cars, so they would receive a check for about 200 pounds from the British Home Ministry in two or three months. He also explained that the taxes had not been paid on the car, hence the O'Douls were expected to sell their old car to provide the funds for the taxes.

The salesman showed them the one car on the lot that was equipped with the 'motorcycle option', and explained that any car that they ordered would be equipped in the same manner. Pilkington took Helen for a test drive and after they returned he took Timothy on the same route. He insisted that Timothy should drive the car for a short distance on a quiet backstreet. Helen drove the car much more than Timothy, because, for one thing, she had a driver's license. Timothy did not. "One does not need a motor vehicle driver's license to drive this car," Pilkington explained. "All you need is a motorcycle license because the car has less than a 50cc equivalent electric engine."

There was considerable discussion between the O'Douls about the color of the new car, and Bryan was not surprised when they chose a red one. Red was an appropriate color for this little car. Pilkington reminded the O'Douls that he would take them home as soon as they returned to the dealership from the train station, and in six weeks their car would arrive from the Continent.

As they were walking over to the train station, Timothy reminded Bryan that he need not have given them this extravagant gift. "I know that," Bryan replied, "but I just wanted to do it, that was all. I like your new car so much that I may just buy one for myself when I get back to Denver."

"You can buy this car in Denver?" Timothy asked.

"I think not," Bryan replied. "But there are electric cars similar to this one that are advertised in the Denver area, and one of them would do nicely for me. I seldom drive out of town now."

"How can we thank you for such a gift?" Helen asked.

"You have already thanked me in many ways," Bryan replied. "You have thanked me with fourteen years of friendship, and I value those years greatly."

ꇔ   ꇔ   ꇔ

Bryan slept all the way from Edinburgh to Heathrow on the special train. When he woke up, people were dragging luggage to the train car exits and Bryan followed suit. He gave his big suitcase to the attendant at the United ticket counter, and meandered over to the 'A' concourse where his plane would be arriving in about an hour. As he rested his eyes in a seat near the entrance to the airplane, one of the United employees came over to him and told him that the plane would depart much later than planned from Heathrow because there was some kind of a security problem over on the 'B' concourse. "However," the employee said, "we will get you to Denver by early tomorrow morning."

Bryan decided to find a telephone and call Carlie. It was almost 9 p.m. at Heathrow but it would be early afternoon in Denver.

"It's me, Carlie. Bryan," Bryan said when Carlie answered the phone. "I am at Heathrow, ready to board the United flight to Denver in the next few hours, but the flight departure has been delayed because of some security problem over on another concourse."

"Thank you for calling," Carlie said. "That probably means you won't get into Denver this evening."

"Right," Bryan responded. "It will be early tomorrow morning."

"How did your visit to the O'Douls go?" Carlie asked.

"It was very nice, and pretty much what I expected," Bryan replied. "But I also learned a lot of things that I didn't know before. For one thing, Timothy has been walking on artificial legs for the past fourteen years, and he never made any mention of that in his letters and emails. He lost all of his right leg and half of his left leg when some Iraqi put a rocket propelled grenade through the side of his Land Rover."

"I wonder why he never mentioned that," Carlie said. "That would cause such a horrific change in one's way of life that you would think that he would say something about it."

"But he didn't," Bryan replied. "The other thing that I found out just yesterday is that Timothy has bone cancer in his left leg and he will be beginning chemotherapy and other treatments next week."

There was a pause at the other end of the line. "And all of this has happened to *one* family?" Carlie asked. "Life doesn't seem to be very fair, is it?"

Bryan had to agree. "Did you get my email message about buying the electric car for the O'Douls?" Bryan asked. Yes, she had.

"I ordered that car just two days ago," Bryan explained, "and then I found that evening that he had bone cancer. The car is equipped with controls for a handicapped person, so both Helen and Timothy will be able to drive the car. They picked 'red' as the color of the car, and the red is really attractive."

"I have that old General Electric stock that must be worth a whole lot more than what the electric car cost me," Bryan said. "I'll cash all that in when I get back to Denver."

"That was very nice of you to do a thing like that for Timothy," Carlie said. "How did you come up with that idea?"

"I saw the advertisement for the car inside the trolleys," Bryan answered. "It's a tiny car, and the battery can be fully recharged overnight. The company that sells the car puts a new 'docking station' in the new owner's garage to make sure that complete recharging occurs over night. The government pays some kind of a stipend for people who buy electric cars here."

"I love you, Bryan Wetherington," Carlie said. "I'm really glad that you continue to do nice things for people – especially people who are having a hard time of it."

"I love you too Carlie Stevens," Bryan said. "I will see you in Denver."

ᑫ৩   ᑫ৩   ᑫ৩

About half way home, flying over the Maritime Provinces, Bryan finally fell asleep in his airline seat. He had a seat next to the window this time, and one of the two seats beside him was vacant. All he could dream about was the life he was experiencing in Denver, his family around him, and especially the woman who filled his life on a daily basis. He knew that the two of them would encounter difficulties as they got older, but for right now they were enjoying a good life. To God that he could have wished some of this good life to Timothy and Helen.

ABOUT THE AUTHOR

Richard Braden is an aeronautical engineer who spent four years in the U. S. Army Field Artillery and seventeen years in U. S. Air Force weapons development. He knows a lot about guns, tanks, artillery, and fighter and bomber aircraft. He has been writing fiction for the past ten years, mostly for teenagers and young adults. He and his wife, Patricia, are both retired from the aerospace industry and live in Lone Tree, Colorado, a suburb of Denver, where Pat is a member of the city council.

Richard can be contacted at 'rbraden@comcast.net'.